"It's safe to say Samantha Bee is the *Girls Gone Wild* version of David Sedaris."
—Seattle Post-Intelligencer Online

"Delightfully neurotic."
—*Nylon Magazine*

"Criminally-entertaining."
—The Daily Beast

"Hilarious." —*Marie Claire*

"A quirky, hilarious addition to the testosterone-dominated world of comedy memoirs." —NPR

. . .—than your wildest dreams." —*BUST*

"Watch your bestseller-list ass, Chelsea Handler." —The Frisky

"It's like reading our own diary, if our diary was way funnier." —Phillyist

"Ridiculously smart, funny, and slightly slutty. As hilarious as her TV work—and even edgier. Sedaris—the NC-17 version." —Philly.com

"[Bee] brings her weird side out for a promenade." —*St. Petersburg Times*

More Praise for
I Know I Am, But What Are You?

"Bee loses nothing in translation to the page."

—*Los Angeles Times*

"Bee successfully brings her witty, self-deprecating, slightly cynical, and semi-scathing world view from screen to page."

—*Publishers Weekly*

"Will certainly please longtime fans."

—*Kirkus Reviews*

"Bee is probing, irreverent and describes the odd imperfections she sees in life with an amazing capacity to hit the nail squarely on its head."

—Seattle Post-Intelligencer Online

"Cheeky."

—*The Globe and Mail* (CA)

"The laughs she generates make this a welcome book."

—*Winnepeg Free Press*

"Funny, and sometimes, vaguely sentimental."

—*Hartford Advocate*

"Humorous."

—*American Way Magazine*

"Conveyed with impeccably dry humor."

—Fox Business

"Easily as funny as David Sedaris."

—Cafemom.com

"Honest and in-your-face."

—SMITHmag.net

"Wickedly funny."

—Eyeweekly.com

"Rather excellent."

—Suicidegirls.com

"Highly recommended."

—NewJerseyNewsroom.com

"Be prepared to chuckle uncontrollably for hours."

—*The Daily Aztec*

**This title is also available
from Simon & Schuster Audio and as an eBook.**

i know i am, but what are you?

SAMANTHA BEE

GALLERY BOOKS
New York   London   Toronto   Sydney

Gallery Books
A Division of Simon & Schuster, Inc.
1230 Avenue of the Americas
New York, NY 10020

NOTE TO READERS
Certain names and identifying characteristics have been changed.

First Gallery Books trade paperback edition February 2011

GALLERY BOOKS and colophon are trademarks of Simon & Schuster, Inc.

For information about special discounts for bulk purchases,
please contact Simon & Schuster Special Sales at
1-866-506-1949 or business@simonandschuster.com.

The Simon & Schuster Speakers Bureau can bring authors to your
live event. For more information or to book an event, contact the
Simon & Schuster Speakers Bureau at 1-866-248-3049 or visit our
website at www.simonspeakers.com.

Designed by Jaime Putorti

Manufactured in the United States of America

10 9 8 7 6 5 4 3 2 1

The Library of Congress has cataloged the hardcover edition as follows:

Bee, Samantha.
    I know I am, but what are you? / by Samantha Bee.—1st Gallery Books
hardcover ed.
        p. cm.
    1. American wit and humor. I. Title.
    PN6165.B44 2010
    814'.6—dc22

                                                              2010002477

ISBN 978-1-4391-4273-8
ISBN 978-1-4391-4274-5 (pbk)
ISBN 978-1-4391-5529-5 (ebook)

To my wonderful family, whom I love dearly,
and especially to my children,
who I hope will never write a book about me.

contents

i know i am,
but what are you?

camp summer fun

Every once in a while I think about what my life would be like if my parents had stayed together and not separated while I was still a baby. Obviously, it would involve a regular commute to the maximum-security penitentiary to visit whichever of them had committed the murder that signaled the official end to their marriage. Something relatively insignificant would have pushed them to the brink. Perhaps my mother wouldn't have been able to tolerate sorting through my father's soiled gym bag to do his laundry one more time, or my father wouldn't have been able to handle my mother's growing interest in founding a pioneer-style ecovillage—whatever the trigger, one of them would have snapped.

The surviving parent would sit happily in their cell, content to be free of the shackles of the doomed relationship, and secure in the knowledge that it had been a justifiable homicide. Their new life would be such a relief that they would dive hungrily into something formerly out of character: a study of medieval French literature or raku pottery classes. Embracing their reinvented self with gusto, they would send misshapen vases and epic poems home at Christmastime, to the bewilderment of their grandchildren. Only the penal system would really blame them for their crime. Anyone who had known them would have thought, *Oh yeah, makes sense. They were a terrible couple. I'm amazed they didn't try to kill each other years earlier . . .*

I come from a long, magnificent tradition of divorce, dating back to the time when nobody was doing it, when it was shameful and nearly impossible to get one. Our family legacy of failed marriage dates back to the era in which women whose behavior vaguely pushed the boundaries of social acceptability were automatically considered either mentally deficient or, more likely, hookers. If you wanted to be an actor, for example, that was just an artsy way of saying, "I do it for money." If you opted to have a job, then you may have been a "career gal" by day, but everyone knew it was probably just a front for your nighttime hookering. And if you dared to get a divorce, then you were indisputably a hooker, and God bless the poor husband who had to put up with you for so long, you horrible floozy.

The women in my family were often suspected of this kind of sluttery, but the glorious truth is that they mostly just loved to marry sadists. Men who liked to beat them up physically or psychologically, drink up all the food money, start a side family, and then proceed to drink up all their new family's food money, too. It was quite a collection of gentlemen that the women on both sides of my family had collectively cast aside. I'm sure they would have endured any tawdry accusations with relish if those accusations had been accompanied by divorce papers.

Dating from well before the turn of the twentieth century, if there has ever been a successful, happy marriage in my family lineage, I have yet to hear about it. When I rack my brain, I can't think of a *single* adult, other than myself, in my immediate or extended family who has not been painfully divorced at least once, usually twice—even the gay ones. This inspires tremendous confidence in my husband.

My maternal and paternal great-great-grandmothers both divorced their husbands, and later went on to marry different kinds of sex perverts; my grandfather left my grandmother for his secretary and her family; my parents got divorced, and their second marriages and/or common-law relationships fell apart; a whole bunch of aunts, uncles, and cousins all split up—which leaves us with a portrait of a shattered family and some very robust hybridized genes. And this is just the tip of the iceberg. After the nuclear winter, all that's going to be left standing are cockroaches and Bees.

Our family tree has been hit by lightning so many times, we're really more of a charred, ungroomed topiary hedge of misfits trying to figure out how we're related. Nobody's really sure what to call anybody else at family gatherings. Are you an aunt? Can I just call you Debbie? Are you a cousin? Oh, so you're related to the lady who was standing in front of the shed during the baby shower? So then . . . am I technically allowed to fool around with your son at the family reunion? Whoops, too late, I already did.

But after all the heartache and confusion, and cousin-on-cousin make-out sessions, getting to have a stepmother like the one I have was the single best result anyone could have hoped for. In keeping with family tradition, my parents threw in the towel when I was an infant, after a long and un-eventful high school romance and subsequent teen preg-nancy. The fact that they followed through with the pregnancy at all seemed to be their own inept form of teen rebellion, though of course, for obvious reasons I'm grateful for it. Although I officially lived with my mother, I saw my dad on weekends, and my grandmother and great-grand-mother were there to fill in the gaps. And though I adored my parents in a way that bordered on adulation, there were many, many of those gaps.

My mother never remarried out of the sheer terror that she would again be saddled with someone like my father. My father, suffering from a similar terror that he would again be saddled with someone like my mother, opted out of the dating pool entirely by marrying her polar opposite. Sensing that there might be a shortfall in the area of competent par-enting, my father was sure that his freshly ratified marriage offered the kind of stability that his child deserved.

It must be terrifying to be thrust into the position of step-parent, but my stepmother, Marilyn, was game and jumped into it full steam ahead with little regard for its perils. I was certainly not the kind of child she was used to, but she seemed confident that she could provide me with the kind of wholesome family experiences almost no one who is *not* a character on a television show has ever had. She exploded onto the scene, breathing a fresh, minty new life into our musty old father-daughter weekends, formerly spent watching NFL games and quietly munching on doughnut holes. Her energy contrasted sharply with what I was used to; she was a busy maker, chatty, industrious, always baking something delicious, pouring vinegar into the dishwasher to cleanse its inner workings, and finding clever uses for leftover *Reader's Digest*s. I was scandalized by the stop-sign patch she wore on the back of her jeans, and desperate for her to give me a Toni Home Perm identical to hers, as I knew only she could.

Though she would have denied it at the time, Marilyn found me peculiar. For one thing, I was exceptionally quiet, though I preferred to think of myself as multifaceted and thoughtful. I was the living definition of the term *indoor kid*. I wasn't technically allergic to the sun or to fresh air, but stepped outside infrequently and gingerly anyway, like a baby vampire learning to survive in the civilian world. I had the complexion of Powder and the muscle tone of a pile of flubber. And since I was basically being raised by senior citizens at the time, my physical activity was limited to driving around the park to look at the trees, driving to the lake to look at the lake, and driving to the mall to look at coats that were "car length."

My grandmother had been raised during the time of polio, so to her, every other child was just an infected mucus machine gunning for her precious only grandchild. On the rare occasions she would actually send me off to the playground, it was always with a laundry list of warnings: "Don't share a comb!" because she was paranoid about lice. "That Stella is a real pimple-hatch; don't go near her face with yours!" "Don't choke to death on your iced [*sic*] cream sandwich—choking is an agonizing way to die." And "Watch out for cars. Before you know it, they'll run over you and drag you down the street to your death, and they won't even have felt the bump." She needn't have worried about me at the playground. All I did was sit in one spot on a bench and count down the seconds before I could reasonably return home and claim that I had played on the teeter-totter with some nit-riddled Pimplestiltskin.

I'm pretty sure my stepmom suspected that *I* thought I was better than everybody else, but actually, what I suffered from was acute and crippling shyness. I was afraid of everything. I wet the bed at night because I was tortured by the fear that I would wake everybody up if I flushed the toilet. I was terrified that other children would speak to me or inflict their halitosis on me. I was afraid to walk across the green shag broadloom because I thought there was a chance it would transmogrify into the Indian Ocean and drown me while my legs were simultaneously being consumed by a hammerhead shark. According to the vast library of shark-death and nautical-disaster literature on my bookshelf, only a few feet of water were required for either. I disliked competition of any kind, because I only liked to win at things and didn't like to try if victory seemed improbable. I would get claustrophobic in public washrooms if they weren't close enough to where people were gathering, because I thought that a pedophile was going to try to snatch me. I slept with a dirty strip of squirrel fur that I had ripped off my grandmother's coat and called my "rat." If I couldn't find my rat, I would sob quietly and moan "Ratty" until my mother fished him out of the garbage again for the last time. I just wanted to hang out with adults and be accepted as one of their own and be let into their adult secret society that included such things as "swearing" and "reading dirty books."

By the time I was seven, my mother and I were living in an old mansion that had been a veterans' hospital during the war and had since been converted into apartments. My mother was dating the owner of the building, and so, to get me out of their hair, they gave me my own dedicated apartment, where I kept all of my toys and records and had my own kitchen. I used to sit up there, in my bell tower of sorts, staring out the window at all the unkempt children playing in the streets, while I ate dry chocolate cake batter with a spoon and listened to my disco records over and over again.

It was an eerie place for such an eerie child to live. Many people had died there, either because of their injuries or, in one case, because of a grisly ax-murder-suicide. As a result, I was besieged by terrible nightmares. When I would descend the long flights of stairs from my apartment to the one my mother shared with her boyfriend, I envisioned axes flying at my head, murderous spirits pursuing me down the hall, body snatchers and cobras lying in wait under the staircase. I lived in fear of being chopped up into little pieces or being buried alive and suffocating to death. Every time I opened a door I thought Nosferatu was going to be on the other side of it ready to suck out all my blood and that Linda Blair would be behind him to telekinetically throw me out a window and finish me off.

So when my stepmother suggested that I was in need of some tepid childhood pastimes, like "tea parties" and "potato sack races," I couldn't even begin to comprehend what she was talking about—she may as well have been speaking Romulan. Except that if she *had* been speaking Romulan, I probably would have understood since I was spending so many warm sunny days inside watching *Star Trek* reruns by myself.

I didn't know how to skate, I didn't know how to swim, I didn't know how to ride a bicycle or socialize, and I didn't care. School "activity days" in the park were an unimaginable source of stress for me. I would spend night after night tossing and turning, imagining myself trying to run to the beanbag with that goddamned egg on the spoon, while I blushed and messed up my team's chances of winning the relay race.

My head was a medical mystery; it not only housed my brain and kept me alive but it was also a genuine soccer ball magnet, as long as the ball was being kicked around by cool teenagers in public spaces. Not only would the ball hit me squarely in the face but those same teenagers would then somehow expect me to return it swiftly and accurately. As the ball flew willy-nilly from my spasmodic kick, I would comfort myself with the knowledge that at least I was amazing at *The Price Is Right* Cliff Hangers game, and that that took the kind of intellect that would serve me better in the future than any mindless sports-ball games.

My stepmother came from a large family and was never afforded the kind of total one-on-one attention that I was used to. When you're the baby in a big group of siblings, you don't get a say in anything. Your mom cuts your hair by putting a bowl on your head and cutting around it with kitchen shears. Sometimes she doesn't even bother dirtying a bowl and just eyeballs it freehand. You have to eat what's on your plate, drink plain white milk, and no one thinks to care whether you like it or you don't. You have to beat your own underpants on a rock down by the river to get them clean, no one will intervene in sibling fights unless someone is bleeding, and if you're a toddler and you want to be fed, you have to push your own high chair up to the table.

Marilyn always tells the story of how taken aback she was when she first met me as a five-year-old girl, and I took a rain check on the green beans she was serving at the table. When she got to me, I said, "Oh, not right now, thank you. I'm actually not fond of those," and assumed that was that. Despite how politely I had declined the green beans, I hadn't realized that I wasn't being given a choice—*not* having them was not an option. I was unaccustomed to this kind of absolutism.

From that point forward, I never understood what was acceptable at my father's house. Why were the preferences and individuality of a child so difficult for them to understand? When I commanded my dual grannies to fetch me a Butterfinger and a ginger ale after a hard day of sticking beans up my nose in kindergarten, they were delivered to me posthaste, right in front of the TV, just where I liked it, so that I could nourish my inner aspect while I watched *The Commander Tom Show*.

As I was shuttled among three houses, I really started to get stressed about the triple life I was leading. I loved my dad and stepmom; I just didn't know how to act when I was at their house. Nobody could figure out what was going on with me, but I kept complaining about stomachaches and nausea as I tried to bow out of various events. I thought I was being really artful, because my technique was to gorge on Sara Lee coffee cake until I felt sick, and then I wouldn't have to lie about not being able to do things. No thinking adult could have missed the sweetly scented frosting torpor that overtook me, paralyzing me in front of my cartoons, sometimes for days at a time. My family doctor prescribed medication for me—a placebo, though I did not know it at the time—that we called "green stuff." I would take it when I was feeling particularly overwrought about something, which was basically every day.

After the intolerable disaster that was my eighth birthday

party—wherein I promptly retreated to my room in hysteri-cal, unstoppable tears as soon as all the children arrived, and sat alone breathing into a paper bag while they enjoyed the festivities—Marilyn had had it. I was an abnormal child and it was time for me to start doing the kinds of things that other children were doing, and loving it. What kind of a child was "allergic to people singing 'Happy Birthday,'" anyway? I needed to be fixed, and early intervention was key. She loved a make-work project, and this was going to be a good one. No more reading inside on sunny days, no more spending summers inside my grandmother's air-conditioned apartment, putting my Barbie dolls in "mature situations" and catching up on my stories. It was off to camp for me! Well, day camp anyway, because my dad and stepmom were also kind of cheap.

The day camp they sent me to was called Camp Summer Fun, which even I as an eight-year-old knew was lame. It was affiliated with the community college where they both worked, and employed college kids who were pursuing ad-vanced degrees in recreational management and leisure stud-ies but who were mainly interested in getting high all day and fucking each other's brains out while we made friendship bracelets in the next room.

I spent most of my time at camp idolizing Adele, the hot-test of the counselors. We all did. The girls were like a little band of tiny helper monkeys who would follow Adele from room to room doing whatever needed to be done. I learned quickly that Adele needed a lot of attention and pampering, so I became the most lethal of the helper monkeys—the alpha helper, if you will—chasing away all the others in service to My Feather-Haired Queen. The other little girls became my sworn enemies, pathetic pretenders to the job.

Clean up the decoupage key-chain station, Adele? No problem! Can I grab you a Capri Sun on the way back? Should I put the needle back on "Hotel California" again, Adele? Can I get your smokes for you? Yes, my nimble kid fingers would *love* to trace the letters of the alphabet across your back while you file your two-inch-long fingernails . . . and might you like to indulge in a finger dip of my cherry Lik-M-Aid? I'd be more than happy to oblige.

When we trucked off as a group to the local pool, I occupied my time running back and forth from the pool to Adele, shuttling handfuls of cool water to splash across her thighs to keep her from overheating. She may not have known my name, but I'm positive that she found me disturbing. I returned from my summer of fun not having learned how to swim or interact positively with other children. I still didn't know how to ride a bike or throw a baseball, but everybody in my family was pretty sure I was gay.

To supplement this highly successful foray into outdoor activities, Marilyn launched a brand-new family tradition—camping trips. She wanted to get me into a more natural setting so that I could learn to appreciate the beauty and majesty of Canada's wonders. In an equally inexpensive way.

We started small, by "rock-and-roll camping" in parking lots and open fields. I'm not sure these expeditions could be

considered outdoorsy, since our tent would end up surrounded by so many cars with their engines running that
it was akin to camping under the exhaust pipe of a Helix
tour bus.

Everyone in Canada seemed to do this. The first (still
cold) holiday weekend of the year meant that everyone
would load up the Trans Am with hot dogs and a pup tent,
and drive until all the cars suddenly stopped in what appeared to be a parking lot edged with trees. Then everyone
would throw their car doors open and blast the music of
BTO into the night sky as they ate beans from a can and
drank themselves blind. Then, although most people would
just end up passing out in their cars, others would crawl fully
clothed into their tiny tents and emerge in the morning,
bleary eyed and still wearing the same outfit, for a bowl of
Froot Loops with some milk that had been left out overnight.
Everyone would spend a bit of time nursing their armpits or
some other random body part that had been third-degree
sunburned from having napped in the sun in a weird way the
day before. And there was always some guy, still drunk from
the night before, fishing around in the campfire ashes for an
uneaten hot dog or two.

We went on these rock-and-roll camping trips for a long
time, until Marilyn could no longer condone them. They
were not making the kind of wholesome impact that had
been the impetus for the journey in the first place. It was
tough baking homemade bread on a hibachi, while all around
us half-naked fat dudes were torching lawn chairs and play-

ing beer bottle baseball as the music from all the car stereos combined into a loud musical maelstrom that you could barely talk over.

So they bought a more substantial trailer, and we began taking real trips to real places that a person might actually want to visit. I was always permitted to bring a friend. In my case, that usually meant bringing my cousin, since no one else really wanted to hang out with me for extended periods of time, but she *had* to because we were related.

Marilyn took camping very seriously. Preparing for a camping trip was a little bit like preparing for the End of Days. Lists were checked and rechecked. Shopping trips were all-day excursions to source out ingredients for complex meals that could still *kind of* be prepared without basic kitchen appliances but with a tremendous amount of effort and a high rate of failure. My father would just tag along or pretend to be thinking up strategies for how to get better fuel economy by reducing the drag on the trailer, for example, when really he was just reading *Penthouse* on the toilet.

Every aspect of the trip was approached strategically, so as to effectively leech all of the excitement out of it long before the actual date of departure. We always had to leave at four o'clock in the morning, for no justifiable reason whatsoever, and our traveling outfits were planned weeks in advance. We ate our predawn meal on napkins so as not to dirty even one last dish before we left the house.

Nobody was ever sure why Marilyn wanted to go camping in the first place because it seemed so contrary to her personality. She had such a meticulous way of running her household, and everything about camping flew in the face of that level of cleanliness. Trailer camping was basically like maintaining a house that you had to drag behind your car, and for someone like Marilyn, that had to be torture. Even worse, all camping-related activities took place outside, where all the dirt was. If we weren't tracking mud into the tent trailer, it was the sand from our bathing suits. Rain brought mold, sloppy eating brought crumbs, and any insect that dared to fly into our little sanctuary would be promptly beaten to the consistency of a dark paste and stuffed in a giant wad of Kleenexes and paper towels.

Also, she hated forest creatures. Not the big, majestic ones but the ones that you actually tend to see on a camping trip: raccoons, bats, mice, and *heaven forfend,* skunks. She disliked their ratlike features, their ratlike love of garbage, and the ratlike way that they scuttled around even though they weren't actually afraid of you at all. If one of them mistakenly wandered into our campsite, it was met with a lot of high-pitched panic and clambering into the trailer en masse to keep our feet out of the way of their rabies. When Marilyn supervised my father's efforts to string our garbage up a tree at night, she wanted it up so high and so precariously placed that none of those creatures would even dare try and get at it. The risks to my father's life were irrelevant.

None of my gloomy idiosyncrasies were welcome on our camping trips. I brought the whole Laura Ingalls Wilder box set of *Little House on the Prairie* books, but that was just to keep up appearances. No longer satisfied by simple stories of families who churned their own butter, I had secretly snuck in a contraband copy of the comic book version of *Alien* with which to terrify myself. At least I could continue the tradition of having horrible nightmares, especially in the middle of the woods where wild creatures like the ones Marilyn feared roamed freely. While she lay there imagining that "forest rats" were somehow embedding their dirty turds into our hammock, I would lie there paralyzed by fear and, with each twig snap, imagine my head getting raped by an alien face-hugger.

I liked to spend most of my time inside the tent trailer, of course, playing quietly by myself, much to the dismay of Marilyn and my father. In the morning, I rarely peed before noon, because it just didn't seem worth it to walk all the way across the grass to the comfort station; besides, I could hold it like a real pro. But everyone grew uncomfortable watching me strain to hold my urine for hours at a time. The edict came down: time to join the land of the living and exit the tent trailer during daylight hours. Even on days that were overcast. Thank goodness I was usually able to play quietly by myself outside just as easily as I had inside.

I have no memory of Marilyn ever sitting down and relaxing on any of our trips. My dad could sit all day in a fugue state, happily staring into the embers of a fire, while Marilyn was busy working her ass off at the idea of enjoying camping. And for her that meant turning out meal after complicated meal on an electric hot plate and a single-burner propane stove. I'd be out in the camping spot playing a rousing game of one-person lawn darts, and Marilyn would emerge from the trailer, covered in carrot shavings, a tennis sweatband around her forehead to keep the work perspiration from dripping into her eyes.

"We're having a vegetarian timpano! Help me turn the crank on the pasta maker!"

They were memorable trips, thanks to her careful planning and meticulous attention to the fun quotient in every destination on the itinerary. If you crossed her, though, you were in the S-H-I-T. None of us ever dared. We did all of our assigned chores without saying a thing. And if you had the misfortune of camping *near* us and you thought that your weekend was going to be a whimsical walk in the park, think again—the nerd campers next to you would turn you in to the park rangers at the slightest infraction without a second thought.

You better dispose of your garbage properly, behave yourself, stop your little dog from barking too much, keep the music down, and don't even *think* about smoking a doobie. Contact highs are *real*, you degenerate. No shenanigans whatsoever after dark, put the guitar away while the child is busy having her nightmares, and no smut mouths will be tolerated.

Violate any of these sacred principles of *our* camping enjoyment, and you would get a visit from the crazy lady next door. She would sneak up on you and scare you as you sat stoned by your campfire, by shining a million-watt flashlight in your eyes and threatening to narc on you. You should take her seriously, because she will take you down if she has to throw you on her back and swim across a lake to the closest ranger station. You don't know what someone this determined is capable of. When you regain your vision, you will see a woman who trudged alone through a cranberry bog in the middle of the night in rubber boots and pajamas, her perm flattened on one side from sleep, with the crazed eyes of a person who has spent the better part of her evening inhaling bleach fumes from trying to scrub a barbecue grill back to its factory shine; while "the man of the house" cowered in the trailer, praying that no one would try to start a fight.

When Marilyn burst onto someone else's campsite, people stood up and listened. Nobody ever *didn't* do as she asked, because no one was ever interested in a second visit. We were the most hated enemies of all the other campers, with our barbecued muffins and eight o'clock bedtimes.

Occasionally, we would go on a camping trip that was more "wilderness" oriented, up to Algonquin Park, for example. We went on paddling trips and nature walks, which were rigorous and beautiful, but we never really got to see any of the wildlife. You could never sneak up on a wild animal with Marilyn in your canoe. You would be paddling too hard to the beat of a Maori call-and-response rowing song she had researched and taught you in the car on the trip up.

Whenever my cousin or any of my friends accompanied us on one of our trips, it took a while for them to get used to her deep reserves of energy and focus. Even as little girls, an as yet undiscovered part of us wanted to seem cute and chaseable to whatever gangly boys were around, camping with their own parents. But when we appeared on-site in our souped-up trailer, our thoroughness alienated us from the other campers. Our campsite was so tidy it looked like the forest floor had been vacuumed; the boys could tell we were going to be too high-maintenance. My friends and I were mortified by Marilyn's shushy ways. And my father was terrified he was going to get his teeth knocked out and secretly wished that he was the one making enough of a ruckus to be on the receiving end of a shush. You could see him look longingly through the trees at the other campers while he tried to concoct some phony moral outrage for the benefit of his wife.

"Hmph. Those people are *animals*. Look at the one with the *big boobs*, there. What a *dumb bunny*. She's gonna start a *forest fire* with all that lighter fluid she's using . . ."

But we were too busy Turtle Waxing the white walls on the Duster to notice.

"Who does she think she's fooling, anyway, with those *big juicy boobs*? Not me! I can spot fake boobs from a mile away! Jeebus H. Krispies—are you *seeing this? Get those things in a proper top. There are children present!* Disgusting. *So* fake. Hanging all out of that bikini top. Let me put on my glasses so I can get a better look."

I never truly appreciated the power of a good shush until the time it saved all of our lives on a wilderness hike that we had undertaken in a remote corner of Algonquin Park. We were finishing up a fairly strenuous four-mile hike when we entered something of an arbor on the way back to our car. We were following a roughly hewn path, but all around us were thick trees and bush so impenetrable and tangled that you really couldn't see into the forest at all. As the rest of us trod lamely along the path, Marilyn forged ahead, guiding the way with her indomitable energy. When she stopped abruptly, we all stopped. And then we heard the sound of a bear. A giant bear, in fact, that seemed to be approximately three inches into the thicket beside us, growling at us in what I think was the most low, menacing sound I have ever heard in my life. We instinctively knew that any animal willing to tolerate the sound of us tromping through the forest jingling our bear bells and singing "Whistle While You Work" was desperate and looking to make a kill.

In an instant, my father and I forgot everything we had been told about how to survive a bear attack and decided instead to surrender ourselves to the creature for immediate dismemberment. I considered the fact that, while my father would make a more *substantial* meal, I would make an infinitely more tender morsel for a hungry animal. But Marilyn had no time to worry about her own inherent deliciousness. She sprang into action, becoming like a wild mother bear herself, circling her cubs, and shushing that angry bear within an inch of its life. She leaned into the arbor.

"HEY! Get away from us! TAKE OFF!"

My father and I were stunned.

"Listen, BEAR. You get out of our G.D. way, OR ELSE."

Nothing was more precious to Marilyn than preserving the illusion of a world without swears, even in the face of death.

"We are GOING TO OUR CAR, AND WE DON'T WANT ANY OF YOUR BUNK."

My stepmother was PG-yelling at the bear like it was a naked frat boy defecating on our campsite picnic table after mandatory lights-out.

"We don't want your silly cub, so GO EAT SOME BERRIES, YOU GREAT LUMBERING B-WORD OF A THING. Come near us, and I will SINGLEHANDEDLY INSERT THIS MEGAWATT FLASHLIGHT WHERE THE SUN DON'T SHINE. THIS IS NOT GOING TO BE COMFORTABLE FOR YOU. Do not MESS WITH ME. I will DESTROY YOU. I am not above TEARING THAT BIG, UGLY HEAD OF YOURS OFF THAT BIG, UGLY NECK and putting it ON MY WALL to hang my PURSE on. PUT THAT in your PIPE and SMOKE IT. Go TO H-E-DOUBLE-HOCKEY-STICKS!"

We clung together in a pack and moved as one down the long, shady corridor to the parking lot, as Marilyn fiercely defended us. Even as my life was being saved, the nerd in me was humiliated and angst-y. What did the bear think of me now? Did she think I was as much of a wiener as I already knew I was? In any case, we didn't camp with much regularity after that event. I suppose everyone had gotten tired of the routine, all the work, all the damp underclothes and

SAMANTHA BEE

unbearable horsefly bites. But still we had the memory of something very special. We were like the keepers of an incredible secret; no subsequent camping trip would ever live up to the electrifying drama of the day Marilyn saved our lives by b-word-slapping an angry bear into submission.

Our camping trips did not "normalize" me—they had no tangible effect on my tentative embrace of nature, and they did not make me any less likely to cry when someone sings me "Happy Birthday." But every so often, when I'm in the quiet darkness of a movie theater . . . and I'm really enjoying whatever it is that I'm watching, and some asshole behind me starts discussing with his giggling girlfriend what he had for lunch that day, I think of Marilyn and her bravery and her inability to suffer fools gladly. Thanks to her and her willingness to trudge across a marsh in her pajamas to scold an entire rugby team high on crystal meth, I am the person I am today.

Yes, I will dive into a satisfying shush without thinking twice. Yes, I am willing to humiliate my husband in this way, even if it means that he will watch the rest of the movie crouched down in his seat and pretending that he does not know me and that I am homeless. But I am not afraid to restore balance to our movie-watching experience in the manner of an angry menopausal woman. In short, yes, I *am* that person in front of you. Now shut up and let me watch my movie. Thank you.

man-witch

For about nine years, from the age of three until I was twelve or so, Jesus was totally my boyfriend. Not my flesh-and-blood boyfriend, of course, but for a *pre*-preteen, it was close enough. I was a patient person; I knew that one day He would make Himself known to me and we would be able to actualize the throbbing *Tiger Beat*–style L-U-V that we felt for each other.

It's not that I wanted to be a nun or anything, au contraire. I was attending a Catholic school at the time, so I knew that living in a convent would mean a lifetime of deprivation and nurse's shoes; besides, half the nuns there looked and smelled like the rejection of life itself. I mean, these were women whose dandruff could settle like coconut shavings on top of their eyebrows and they wouldn't even notice. The other half were just plain mean, and clearly savored the terrifying effect they had on people. You could see that they had all their lady parts, but you just knew that once a month they menstruated dust. Who would want to join a club like that?

So I didn't need to be a bride of Christ. I was comfortable just dating Him, and if things got a little more serious, then that was cool, too. But one thing was certain. He and I were *together*. When I talked to Him, it was as intimate as if I had picked up my Hot Lips phone and dialed directly to His condo in Heaven.

I had a notebook dedicated to ironing out the details of my postmarital name change. Samantha Christ. Mrs. Jesus Christ, Lamb of God. Mrs. Samantha H. Christ. I didn't know what the *H* stood for, but whenever my father took the Lord's name in vain, he always added it for some reason, and I thought it gave everything a nice rhythm. In fact, Jesus and I were so tight that, if at any moment He should materialize, I knew we would listen to my disco records and eat Tang straight from the package, just like lovers did. I was ready.

Jesus was everywhere I looked at school—hanging on the walls, pictured in my books, overseeing my hand washing at the miniature sink, casting a benevolent eye on me as I spray-painted the Christmas angels I had made from old L'eggs containers. My Catholic school was considered *progressive,* which meant that *my* Jesus wasn't blood soaked and scary, hanging from the cross with His eyes rolled back into His head in the final agonizing release of His life force—though there was a place in my heart for that guy, too.

My Jesus was cool. He looked like Kris Kristofferson circa *A Star Is Born*, only with penetrating blue eyes and a nonthreatening admiration for children that I, as a child, both understood and appreciated. He wore a freshly pressed robe all the time, but you knew He had a great ass and could have pulled off a pair of jeans and worn-out cowboy boots, even if you weren't sure why you would want that.

Jesus had nice big, rough hands with clean fingernails, so you knew that He could chop down a tree if He had to, but that He could also handle a kitten with tenderness. He had a lustrous but well-maintained chestful of hair, because as the Son of God, He was bound to be hairy only in all the right places. As if Jesus would have little stray sprouts on his shoulders or the bridge of his nose—unthinkable!

I'd picture myself lying beside Jesus in a field of sweetgrass, my fingers entwined in His chest hair in a nonsexual way. We'd laugh and talk, and I'd wash His feet with exotic oils and then dry them with my hair. I never questioned it. It was just what you did when you were with Jesus.

Of course, Jesus was *Jesus*, and that meant He could be unpredictable, too. He was always on the verge of materializing in some crazy place—you never knew when or where. A person had to be prepared to get down on their hands and knees and wash and dry those precious Jesus feet. And I was.

I'd play a game with myself as I walked down the street. "If Jesus appeared to me *right now*, where would I get a big bowl to put His feet in?" I'd wonder. "If I go into that diner, would they lend me a dish towel for Him to sit on so that He doesn't sully His robe?" I'd challenge myself to see Jesus in all the panhandlers. "What if that guy in the poo-stained tracksuit was Jesus? Could I *really* dry His feet with my hair?" Of course I could—as soon as His Jesusness was definitively proven by way of either (a) careful inspection of His crucifixion wounds, or (b) some kind of unearthly glow, possibly, hopefully, in the form of a halo.

Jesus was no slouch. When He sang to me, which He often did in my girlhood fantasies, He always sounded a bit like Kenny Loggins, another bearded dude I was quite fond of, most likely because he reminded me of Jesus. And I loved that He had a temper. I mean, most of the time He was quite levelheaded, but when He banished those merchants from the temple in a fury, that's when I knew that He was real husband material. Not that He would be violent with me, but because the fact that He could get a bit hot under the collar meant that He was passionate, a bit of a roughneck, the kind of guy who would defend my honor, as required.

It didn't hurt that His representative in my life was a smoking-hot priest at school named Father Andy. With Jesus busy elsewhere, Father Andy was a suitable flesh-and-blood substitute for my affections. He didn't have Jesus's sexual magnetism, but he wore robes all the time and looked enough like Peter Frampton to make an impression.

Father Andy's laissez-faire attitude was supposed to "turn us on" to Christ in a fresh, hip, nonjudgmental way, but in the end turned us on to something completely different, including jealousy. Fancying myself the only girl in class mature enough to handle a long-term relationship, I was shocked when all of the other girls simultaneously discovered cosmetics the moment Father Andy started coming into our classroom. One day, I walked into class, and all of these formerly fresh-scrubbed girls were wearing shimmery pink lip glosses in various shades of whore. The boys tried to impress Father Andy, too, with their knowledge of choke holds and physical restraints. Within minutes of his arrival, all of the boys would suddenly be on the floor in Greco-Roman wrestling positions, sweating and grappling with one another as Father Andy looked on casually.

It was a sexually confusing time for the girls and the boys alike, but I secretly knew that I was above it. All of that other stuff was just child's play. My path to his heart, I figured, would be through my intelligent questioning of the faith. I thought that if I just asked the right philosophical questions, I would impress Father Andy with my worldliness, and then we would hug each other tightly and run away from the church together to raise baby rabbits for a living.

When we were asked to write about our faith, I specifically indicated that I didn't believe in some bearded man sitting upon a throne in Heaven with angels all around Him, which I thought made me seem edgy and cool and would make me stand out. Unfortunately, since I literally believed that God was a bearded man sitting upon a throne in Heaven with angels all around Him, I didn't have much to say when Father Andy asked me to elaborate. "I mean, sitting in a *chair* with *angels* all around Him? I think God would find that a bit *boring,* don't you?" I was really grasping at straws. "I mean . . . why would He *sit* when He obviously possesses *the power of flight* and the ability to hurl . . . lightning bolts . . . at stuff? There's no way He'd just sit around when He is capable of levitating and smiting things. That would be ridiculous."

My best opportunity to impress him, I figured, would be at our annual church retreat, a two-day overnight camping trip on the grounds of a Catholic fat camp called Camp Mshuk-wuk, which, loosely translated, means "cows" in Mohawk. I pulled out all the stops—my red satin jacket with the ice cream cone patch, my rattiest and therefore most read miniature picture-Bible, and even though I didn't need it, an inch-thick application of Bonne Bell Dr Pepper Lip Smacker lip gloss to ensure that I was closed-mouth kissable.

Titillated beyond belief, I tried to look casual when Father Andy smoked a cigarette and drank a glass of wine around the campfire. A *cigarette*? What a *dirty birdy*! But on the outside I was as cool as a cucumber. Who among us *didn't* enjoy unwinding with liquor and smokes in the company of unsupervised children?

Imagining myself leagues beyond the other children, I couldn't let my exhilaration show, and spent most of my time keeping his ashtrays clean and replenishing his Blood of Christ . . . until I realized that Father Andy had no intention of leaving the priesthood for me. In fact, he seemed to have a very hard time remembering my name. Even after I blithely posited the question of whether he thought it was possible that God might be a *woman*—an absurd idea that I thought might just be original enough to capture his attention—he barely noticed me at all.

Stung by his ability to resist me (I mean, *how did he do it?*), I grew tired of being his bottomless glass. I decided to tell my mom that my beloved priest was just a washed-up booze hound, you know, to give her the opportunity to agree with me, but incredibly, she took his side. "A *glass* of wine? God, I hope he was smoking something a little stronger than *tobacco*. Poor fag. I should introduce him to Carl . . ."

She thought that any member of the priesthood who was passably handsome was just an adorable, closeted homosexual who would benefit from exposure to Carl, one of her many fun, freewheeling gay friends. I had no idea what she was getting at.

No matter. Jesus understood that we had obstacles to overcome in our long-distance relationship, and I dove back in with a refreshed sense of purpose. I had already read *The Thorn Birds,* so I knew what I was getting myself into. It would be difficult for Jesus to take time away from being the Son of God, but in my case, it would be worth it. I was willing to wait for Him. We could spend our days innocently rolling around on the beach and caressing each other mournfully, knowing that the requirements of His job would make it impossible for us to ever consummate our love. Thankfully. Because even though I knew all about sex, and by that time my Barbies were all swinging naked from the chandeliers, I personally still found it revolting.

It wasn't easy being so Catholic around my parents. They were forcefully nonreligious, but they hadn't really been in the picture when my grandmother had done all the decision making about my education. If either of them had had their way, I would have gone to the Atheist School for the Children of Heretics and Pagans.

My father couldn't even talk about religion without lighting up like a Christmas tree—an angry one that would spit razor-sharp needles, spark up, and burn the house down, taking everyone with it. Once he got started, you couldn't stop him. He referred to all religious people as "Jeebus Freaks" and "TMRs" (which stood for The Mentally Retarded). Then he would feel guilty for a second and soften a little. "I mean, it's not their *fault* they're so stupid. I feel sorry for them, I really do. Dolly Dimwits." He may not have cared if we all went to Hell, but he definitely cared about not being caught by my stepmother swearing in the presence of a child.

And then he would ramp up again: "Why not just believe that Goldilocks and the Three Bears were Jeanus's [sic] siblings?" He thought that calling Jesus "Jeanus H. Cripes" or "Jeebus H. Crackers" was hilarious. "Let me ask you something. What was God's inspiration for creating fondue? Did He get tired of eating all of those sea creatures and birds? Poof! Let's dip some bread into a cauldron of melted cheese! Mmm, delicious! Way to go, God!"

As a Jeebus Freak myself, I did not appreciate his sarcasm. But as a model Catholic, I turned the other cheek and chose to take the high road, quietly praying for a cure for his heathenism. Failing that, I prayed that he wouldn't get smoted [*sic*] too hastily, and I decided to keep the magnitude of my secret love for Jesus on a need-to-know basis.

My parents imagined that, given the opportunity to make my own decision about my faith at a much later age, I would ultimately decide to reject religion entirely, as they themselves had done. But as it turned out, at the age of seven I was eager to be baptized. Thanks to the movie *Jaws*, which my stoner cousin had snuck me into, I had developed an intense fear of dying and knew for sure that it was imminent. I knew there was no way I was going to make it to my eighth birthday and I didn't want to end up boiling in my own skin courtesy of the devil.

Jesus and I were going steady by that time anyway, so it was time to make things official. My grandmother was thrilled, her joy tempered only by the extreme embarrassment of having had an unbaptized child in the household for so long. We kept the ceremony from my father because we were afraid that he would lay an egg if he knew about it. So there I was, resplendent in the family tartan, transforming into an ultra-Catholic before my grandmother's tearful eyes and my mother's horrified ones.

Ever since I could remember, my mother had found my religiousness charming and slightly alien. She didn't rally too hard against it at first, but every time she came into my room, she shuddered at the sight of Jesus, his picture tacked to the wall above my bed, holding His robe open to reveal His sacred heart entwined with a crown of thorns and emitting a single drop of blood.

My mother playfully insisted that, given His provenance, Jesus would have more likely been swarthy (maybe even a little bit black!) than silken haired and ethereally pale with luminous blue eyes. More Cat Stevens than Kris Kristofferson, then. She described the lack of hygiene in His time, implying that He probably would have been unwashed and slightly smelly, not strawberry-scented and manscaped the way I imagined Him. Since I had an extreme paranoia about dirty feet and walking barefoot, I didn't appreciate her assertion that Jesus most likely didn't have shoes and that the soles of His feet were tough and black. Or her notion that He probably didn't even speak English!

The official name she gave Him was "sweaty bohunk," which was specifically designed to piss off my grandmother, since that's what *she* liked to call taxi drivers and gardeners. I ignored my mother completely and threw myself deeper into my religious training, preparing to receive sacrament number two, Communion. My grandmother and I went shopping for a pattern for the perfect dress, which we were having custom-made with loads of glamorous white marabou trim. I took extra classes, learning all about the Body and Blood of Christ, and raised money for the Catholic children of Guatemala by selling candies and Jesus-themed candles. Only for the Catholic children, though.

My mother decided to pull out the big guns. She was determined to open my mind if she had to jam a crowbar in there and physically pry the two halves of my brain apart. It was time to introduce me to her religion of choice—Wicca.

I didn't know anything about her faith, other than the fact that it was something my grandmother couldn't bear to think about and that it involved congregating somewhere on the wrong side of the tracks. All I had seen of it up to that point involved rubbing special oils on various amulets and running out from time to time to bathe pebbles and seeds in the light of the full moon. I suspected that it was evil on some level, but I was willing to let it slide for the sake of my mother.

For reasons nobody could fathom, she decided that the best thing to do would be to bring her eight-year-old, super-Catholic daughter into a dark room full of white witches to witness the union of two members of the coven. The coven met once a week above a store that sold Wiccan supplies and magick bath salts to the lovelorn.

To say that I was out of my element would be the understatement of the century. From the moment I entered the building, I felt that I was under siege and that by the end of the evening Satan would be tap-dancing his way into my heart with his little goat hooves, stealing me away from Jesus for good. I fingered the St. Jude medallion I had slipped into the pocket of my jumper and started praying.

Everyone ran to the door to greet us, delighted by the

exciting prospect of heathenizing an eight-year-old. I was paralyzed with fear. It was like looking at the cast of *The Pirates of Penzance*, as costumed by a sixth-grade home economics class. Head scarves, knickers (for those who chose to wear pants), men in billowing blouses, women in hand-sewn dresses festooned with multiple belts to hold up their pendulous breasts, unencumbered by bras. A man in a homemade Sprout costume and cowboy boots sauntered by, his testicles dangling below the peekaboo-length dress he had crafted out of felt. With all of the shirt cocking going on, there sure was a lot of graying genitalia on display. I guess foundation garments were not required by any of the Wiccan commandments carved into their sacred stone tablets.

We were, however, all required to take off our shoes and socks, which I found disgusting. Instantly choking back tears, I looked at all of those dirty feet whose juices were soon to be mingling with mine. And as soon as I did, I felt certain that someone had cast an athlete's-foot hex on me. My feet tingled with fungus just thinking about stepping down onto that flatbed of foot disease.

And then he appeared. The Man-Witch.

At about seven feet tall by four feet wide, he material-ized in the doorway in his purple crushed-velvet robe, with a crooked walking stick in one hand and a joint in the other. His body hair was so unkempt and his eyes so wild, he looked vaguely Cujo-like but smelled sweet, like san-dalwood mixed with pot. From everyone's hushed tones, I could tell he was the Big Enchilada of the coven. His real name was Robert, but his "craft name" was Sun-Thorn. I called him the Man-Witch.

My mom beamed when she saw him and gave me a little shove toward him. He swiftly entered my personal space and greeted me warmly. I interpreted this to mean that my virgin body was to be sacrificed to Satan momentarily, and so I silently prayed even more fervently to Jesus for protection. I prayed as we all entered the sacred space and found a place to sit on the pentacle made of masking tape. I prayed as they sprinkled grass seeds behind our backs and recited incantations about nature and the spirits in the trees. I prayed as they passed a cup from lip to lip, and prayed as I refused to drink from it for fear of the cold-sore incantation that was probably swirling around inside; I was not having any part of it. And when they turned off all the lights to celebrate the sacred union of two of the coven's membership in "Satanic Partnership" (or so I thought), I prayed hardest of all, tears slipping down my cheeks, as the two lovebirds joyfully ran around our circle, jumping over the broomstick and the cauldron of fire.

Amid this flurry of activity, I had questions. Would Jesus think that I was cheating on Him by being here, or would He be able to look into my heart and know that my intentions were pure? What if I accidentally said Satan's name three times in my head? Does just *thinking* about Satan *really* invite him into your heart, or do you have to personally invite him the way you have to do with vampires? And does it count if you say Satan's name three times in one paragraph like I just did, or is nonconsecutive usage okay?

Whatever the answers to these many-fold questions, it was at that point that I agreed to devote my life to service if I were to make it out alive. In Catholic-speak, that meant caring for lepers and taking handicapped people grocery shopping. I hoped for the latter but didn't dare pray for that on top of everything else.

I ran through a list of all my sins up to that point. I was sorry that I had tried to rat out Father Andy for the sin of enjoying a glass of wine from a box. I shouldn't have pretended to "accidentally" drop my clog from the third floor of the mall when I totally did it on purpose and *actually* wanted it to fall on someone's head. And it was *not* my place to suck all the chocolate off the almonds intended for the Guatemalan children's rescue mission, and then force my grandmother to pay for them anyway.

Up to that point in the Wiccan wedding ceremony, I had effectively concealed my terror. Everyone interpreted my silence as shyness and let me have my own contemplative space. But when the metal tub came out, it was game over for the little religious zealot in the cowl-neck sweater. Was it going to be death by drowning, or was the tub just a catch basin for the bloodletting, which I assumed they would be ecstatically smearing all over themselves after I was gone? I burst into sobbing tears; the floodgates were open. This was it, I thought, time to climb into the tub and accept my fate!

But actually, it was time to bob for apples.

I refused the apple bob, just on principle. It seemed too much like frenching and I didn't really need to be swapping spit with pagans. Especially since so many of them had dipped their straggly beards in the water by then.

My mother rolled her eyes at me. She had been watching me on the verge of collapse the whole time, and wondering how someone as cool as she was could have spawned someone as uptight as me. Even I started to feel like a bit of a drip as I took in the smiling faces of my mother's witchmates. They may not have been conventionally minded. They may have looked like a ragtag bunch of misfits, huddled together in communal rejection of their parents' values and the wearing of pants. But at least they had one another, and maybe for them, that was enough. With Satan nowhere in sight, I had to ask myself, Would Jesus really condemn these people to Hell for all eternity just for not believing in Him?

The answer, of course, was yes. But at least I was no longer afraid of them.

Afterward, there was a potluck to celebrate the wedding of the happy couple. Everyone brought either Swedish meatballs still in the saucepan or a box of doughnuts, like we did. I was unimpressed with the spread, but everyone else seemed really excited, so I helped myself to a couple of Boston creams anyway.

The members of the coven gave the couple a sacred, wizard-looking thing, which I have to assume was a bong, and ushered them out to a van parked on the street that had blackout curtains and twenty minutes left on the meter. No one wanted to say the words *fuck-mobile*, but that's what it was. Everyone found my naïveté adorable.

The Man-Witch had changed into jean shorts and a Coors Light T-shirt by then, and he chatted with my mother for a while about seeds and stuff. Then everyone started exchanging herbs and plants that they had force rooted for one another. It went from being a dangerous and seamy den of iniquity to a *Good Housekeeping* coffee klatch in five seconds flat. They were *abnormally* normal. It seemed like the only requirement for membership in the Wicca club was a green thumb and a raging desire to feel like part of something counterculture. In fact, they were downright boring.

As my fear of imminent death dissipated, I started to rethink the commitment I had made to full-time Catholic service. Sure, I still dreamed of the possibility that Jesus would come to Earth and tickle my back nonstop for an hour and a half while I made Him a lanyard. But wasn't it enough to be Jesus's girlfriend from afar? I had His ear. Maybe I could just put in a good word for the lepers. I wasn't much good to anyone if I contracted leprosy myself anyway. That night I prayed to Jesus for the last time. I prayed for the wayward souls of those happy Wiccans that they would someday see the value of a well-worn pair of corduroys. I prayed for the lepers that they would still have legs to slip into their flannel pajama bottoms. And I prayed that my mom would buy me the Sergio Valente jeans I so desperately needed to lure my secular crush, Joey, into the closet for seven minutes in Heaven so I could get closer to first base and to my main squeeze JC at the same time.

WWJD? It's arrogant to think that mere mortals can decipher the mind of Jesus. But if I had to guess, I'm pretty sure He'd totally approve of the jeans.

the birds and the bee

There aren't many things I know for sure, but I feel pretty confident about this one: You should never tag along on someone else's honeymoon. And if you do, you definitely shouldn't bring your kids. I know this because my dad and stepmom crashed their best friends' honeymoon with me and one of my pale and unenthusiastic friends in tow. I mean, who does that?

We were scheduled to go to the Maritimes on one of our patented type-A camping trips, but our painstakingly prepared vacation dossier was still a work in progress. My parents' friends—let's call them Bob and Donna—must have mentioned in passing that they would be honeymooning there and we should all meet up. An invitation, I'm sure, that was both halfhearted and insincere. The same way you might say, "We should all go out for Chinese food sometime," or "Thank you for the show!" which is really just a polite way of saying "That show was terrible and you were terrible in it, but thank you for going to the trouble of performing it!" I'm also quite positive that at no time was it presented as an invitation to join in for the entire length of their honeymoon.

No matter to my father! It was as if Jeebus H. Christ Himself had emerged from a burning bush and deposited into his hands a solid gold tablet engraved with a diamond-studded invitation. Why the hell *wouldn't* we go? And for that matter, why not make it a sixsome? We were camping, they were staying in a motel . . . what a terrific opportunity for all of *us* to grab a nice hot shower and maybe catch a football game on the boob tube! Maybe up to three! One right after the other!

Even at the tender age of nine, I felt awkward as my dad and stepmom enthusiastically dragged us to every event on the itinerary of their best friends' postnuptial Maritimes extravaganza. I mean, it's not like anyone would plan a trip out east without stopping at the *Anne of Green Gables* house to learn about old-timey bread baking, so why *not* carpool? We did everything with the newlyweds—lobster boils, clambakes, whale watching, fish-themed photo ops—all of it taking place with one giant elephant looming in the room at all times; namely, that the moment we were out of sight, Bob and Donna would be up in each other's genitals within about five seconds flat.

Never before or since have I felt so acutely unwanted.

My friend, of course, was oblivious to the impropriety of the whole endeavor, as she sprawled across their pathetically underused marital bed and pored over every last detail of the emergency *Josie and the Pussycats* collection we had brought along for rainy days. (And it rained almost every day.) There is nothing on Earth less conducive to lovemaking than the sight of two greasy-haired nine-year-old children quietly fighting over the last piece of fudge in matching VIRGINIA IS FOR LOVERS satin jackets. Whenever the two of us got together, we had that weird kid smell that is reminiscent of Bubblicious but in the end is just the odor of unwashed clothes and sour prepubescent armpits. Innocent, but also gross.

I remember that vacation like it was yesterday . . . Bob's eyes boring a hole in my skull as I got up to pour myself the last of his Cokes, leaving a trail of Bugles crumbs behind me large enough to have nourished a stranded Argentinean soccer team through some tough times. And Donna shuddering as we stoically refused her offer of Kleenex to blow our snotty noses, preferring to reinhale our rattling boogers at annoyingly irregular intervals.

It was the death of sex. No one could do it. And no one could really do the things that would have made it okay *not* to be doing it, like smoking pot and telling racist jokes, seventies-style.

When we weren't numbing our tender skin in the freezing waters of the Atlantic Ocean or pillaging the all-you-can-eat cold lobster tables at the church picnic we crashed, we watched a lot of television in their motel room. At the time, women's tennis was a big deal. Lots of drama and high stakes. Even for non–tennis-playing Canadians who were busy tagging along on their soon-to-be-ex-friends' honeymoon.

And so there we were, inside on yet another Maritimes gray day, watching the Wimbledon ladies' singles quarterfinals, a hard-fought battle between the Lady Titans of Tennis, Chris Evert and a certain Miss Billie Jean King, when it happened .. The Slip Up.

In the heat of sexual frustration, his tongue loosened by liberal consumption of Canadian Club and warm Tab, Bob uttered the words that shattered our vacation bliss. He called Billie Jean King a "carpet muncher."

The sudden intake of breath in the room was audible, all oxygen sharply inhaled by my father and my stepmother. They were certain that this was the first time my girlfriend or I had ever heard smutty language in our short lives. We were only nine. We were barely toilet trained, right?

The tone of the evening went from pleasantly drunk to stone-cold sober. The TV was turned off. Multiple cigarettes were extinguished. The axis of the Earth shifted incrementally under our feet. Code Red. Situation Not Normal. Crisis-Stage-Extreme-Danger. Threat Assessment DEFCON One, Involving Imminent Sex Talk With A Minor.

My stepmother's eyes, instantly rimmed with red, looked like a pair of saucers spinning in her head. She wordlessly commanded my father to: *Fix. This. Situation.* Donna exchanged a look with her husband that said, *I was planning to have sex with you, but now I'm just mad.* And Bob shot us a look that said, *Get the fuck out of my room. I'd like to have angry sex with my wife now.*

But instead, my father sat us down for an explanation of lesbianism . . .

"You know how 'work Jackie' always wears really sensible shoes—"

My stepmother interrupted him, her voice breathless and about three octaves higher than it would normally have been, and her eyes glittering with promise. There was a thought bubble above her head that seemed to say, "I'm *doing* it. I'm really *doing* it! We're having *The Talk*!"

"Sometimes . . . when a woman . . . loves another woman . . . who isn't her husband . . . No, cancel that. A lady sometimes doesn't want to marry a man. She wants to marry a lady. And then one of them is the *lady* lady, and one of them is the *man* lady. Tennis players are different . . . sometimes. Also, lady field-hockey players sometimes don't like boys. I mean, they like boys, but they don't *like* like boys. Oh, gosh . . . Remember the time we went for brunch and we saw that lady who sort of had a beard . . . ?"

I was mortified, and looked over at my girlfriend to see if this was all registering with her, but she was too busy daydreaming to notice the runaway train that was thundering through the motel room. She hadn't spoken a single word to any of the adults so far on the trip, and even when she occasionally spoke to me, it was in such an eerily quiet tone that only a nine-year-old girl or a dog could hear it. I'm pretty sure that Bob and Donna thought she was a deaf-mute, albeit one who could miraculously sense the vacuum seal breaking on a can of Pringles from a mile away.

I was eager to let the whole thing go, when my friend asked casually, "But what's munching the carpet got to do with anything?" All the clocks in the room simultaneously stopped ticking. Of all the times to pipe up, why had she chosen *this* as her first foray into conversation territory? Why now? There had been plenty of excellent opportunities up to that point. Where had *she* been when my parents were debating a diversion to the world's longest covered bridge, in lieu of an extensive tour of the region's plentiful french fry–based snack trucks? Thanks to her indifference, I had had to watch my dream of a fried potato smorgasbord vanish into thin air, while we ate soggy egg sandwiches by the side of the road and stared at a bridge all day. I would remember this. After a long sigh, my father's shoulders visibly sagged under the heavy burden he was about to lift.

Desperate not to scar us for life or encourage us to pursue alternative lifestyle choices, my parents knew they were in the shit. This was it. The heart of darkness. They were about to explain the fundamentals of lesbian sex to two impressionable nine-year-olds, and they had to do it in such a way that minimal information would be supplied but no further questions would arise. There was no going back until the job was done. But first, as a prelude, they would have to explain the *regular* facts of life to put everything in the proper context.

My father was as red in the face as if he had just swallowed a scorpion and it was stinging him from inside his throat. It was partially from having to explain sensitive material to us but *mostly* from having to do so with the knowledge that he was missing precious television time. My stepmother appeared to have inhaled the contents of a helium balloon, her voice so thin and so high that like my girlfriend's, it was barely audible to human ears: "When a man . . . and a woman . . . want to make a baby, they *make love* . . . which is to say, that the man's penis goes into the lady's vagina and he basically, um, lays an egg inside of her that becomes a baby eventually." My father chimed in, helpfully: "But when two ladies want to make love . . . it's like two doughnuts bumping up against each other, and then they munch each other's rugs."

My friend was disgusted by this, and turned away, done. I sat, paralyzed with fear that this conversation would continue even one nanosecond further.

"Clear?"

I nodded vigorously.

I didn't want to tell them, because I didn't want them to feel bad about having missed the opportunity to teach me something, but I was already quite acquainted with the regular facts of life, and perhaps even more so with some of the *ir*regular facts of life. My mother was fixated on the notion that it's unhealthy to prolong childhood innocence past the age of, say, seven. Trying to toughen me up, she routinely mocked me for my devotion to disco music and my childhood ambition of becoming Kate Jackson. Whenever I was at her place, she was happy to let me do the grocery shopping and cook dinner on my own for both of us while she was out. I took the subway to school by myself, got myself to bed at a time I thought an adult would approve of, and shopped for all my own clothing. Naturally, this meant that I had free rein to choose my own outfits for school, which produced many near heart attacks on the part of my grandmother, who also happened to be the secretary at the Catholic school I attended. White short-short suede hot pants, black nylons (with reinforced toes), and a pair of open-toed high-heeled clogs, for example, on the first day of first grade.

My self-directed ensembles were usually some confused attempt to combine the uniforms of the Dallas Cowboys cheerleaders with the somber aspect of a Portuguese widow. Whenever my mother prepared lunch for me, which was sporadic, it usually meant slapping last night's leftovers onto canapé crackers and throwing them into a Baggie to be sorted out later, presumably by me. Imagine my surprise when I opened my lunch box one day to find that the extremely rare roast beef my mom had prepared the night before had exuded so much blood into the plastic wrap that my sandwich looked like an IV bag I was planning to administer for lunch. Well, at least it drew people's eyes away from my outfits for a while. My report card read "Cries easily."

One evening, as I carefully prepared my dollies for bed with their silky pajamas and pin curls, my mom literally threw a little red book at me from across the room with a "Here. Read this. Let me know if you have any questions." It took me about half a day to get through, and afterward, oh, did I have questions. The book contained the most explicit descriptions of every sexual proclivity in existence—I had a *lot* of questions:

"Is it the man that pees on the woman or the woman that pees on the man?"

"What if you forget your safe word?"

"Do we have any shlurp bars in Toronto?"

"What's *your* safe word?"

"What if you go to shrimp someone and they haven't washed their feet?"

"What should *my* safe word be? Is *alphabet soup* too obvious?"

Soon, not only was I familiar with the basics of male-female sexual intercourse, I could explain in great detail what bukkake was. I could give you the rundown on a Cincinnati Bowtie, or perhaps even take you through the intricacies of a German Scheisse video. So a year later, a simple carpet munch between two robust female athletes held little mystery for a savvy youngster like me.

Also, my mother had several gay male friends who were *unbelievably* daring and promiscuous, it being the late seventies and all. They would come over for dinner and regale us with tales of their sexual conquests, which were many and varied, and seemed to have all the impact on their lives of an itchy mosquito bite or a really satisfying sneeze. Carl was into nipple clamps and cock rings, while Keith was more of a fisting kind of guy. But they seemed willing to do it any which way with just about anyone who entered their eye line and gave them a lingering look. I'll never forget the day we sat around the kitchen table eating spaghetti and meatballs, which I had made, as Carl described to me the practice of autoerotic asphyxiation. As I cradled my gerbil, Pierrepont, tightly in my hand, I felt my childhood officially end.

The peripheral benefit of all this knowledge was a sharp uptick in playground popularity. *Star Wars* role-play was the game of choice in our neighborhood, but it was frustrating for me to be the only one who had actually seen the movie. I had spent many a recess trying to explain the fine points of the plot to my slack-jawed third-grade cohorts, only to hear infuriating cries of "Fetch me the Siberian Emerald!" from the fat kid playing Uncle Owen. I tried to reason with them, but in the end, they played the game they wanted and certainly never let me play the coveted role of Princess Leia. When everyone was sick of hearing me bitch about how poorly they were doing things, I was usually relegated to playing R2D2 and speaking in bleep-blop-bloops in my quest for vérité.

But armed as I was with knowledge of water sports and necrophilia, *Star Wars* role-play took on a whole new meaning.

Suddenly Princess Leia and Luke Skywalker were a whole lot more knowledgeable about each other's bodies. If only we'd known then that they were actually brother and sister! That would have gotten them talking back on Tatooine! Who knew that Dark [*sic*] Vader was such a freak for

B&D! Although, to be fair, his gimp mask was something of a dead giveaway. And Chewbacca. I mean, I was pretty sure there was *something* off about his relationship with Han Solo, but once I realized they were both into Furries, it all started to make sense.

The children on the playground began to rely on my breadth of perverted knowledge to spice up our below-average games. Soon I had graduated from my nonspeaking role as the unattractive midget robot and been promoted to the position of "rarely speaking robot who executive produces the playground." No matter. Whatever tertiary character I had been assigned would end up with the most spectacular kink of all. Remember that scene in the movie when C3PO mounts all the dead Jawas? Of course you don't.

Sadly, even with all of these ideas coursing through my head, the thing that really disgusted me more than anything was plain old French kissing. I mean, it's one thing to run around dumping chocolate pudding down the back of your lover's diaper as foreplay, but to look him straight in the eye and stick your tongue in his mouth? That's unhygienic and just plain ridiculous. And because of that, I flat-out refused to expose my Barbies to it.

I did, however, subject them to a range of sexual situations that would have turned anyone's parents' hair white if they had stood and listened outside the door for more than three consecutive seconds.

There were six main players in my coterie of dolls: G.I. Joe (macho, good-looking), Wonder Woman (hot carpet-munching neighbor, not interested in G.I. Joe, busy with athletics), Marie Osmond (career gal, smart, brunette), Ken (gay, obviously), regular Barbie (slutty, dumb, eternally single), and an old-timey Barbie from the sixties with a bouffant hairdo (smoker's cough, swinger).

Naturally, everybody in town was divorced and self-employed, with loads of spare time for their standing appointment with afternoon delight. At any one time, you might find my doll collection in multiple ménage à trois in the Barbie Dream House. Obviously, G.I. Joe possessed the only feasible penis in town, but you could always count on Ken to be looking on and jerking off in the corner. Nobody was too hot for bouffant Barbie either, but she was keen to participate and would always do nice things, like make sure everybody had enough snacks to keep their energy up and plenty of lemonade for hydration.

Everyone was nude most of the time, and when they weren't, they were largely festooned with what appeared to be bedsheets fashioned into easy-access togas. It was basically like *Caligula* in there. Mostly they spent their time hopping in and out of one another's beds, getting caught cheating, having long, laborious conversations about honesty, switching partners, and getting caught cheating again. Also, they adored the music of Fleetwood Mac and would routinely hold naked dance parties out on the Barbie sundeck.

Everyone in my family thought my love of my Barbies was fanciful and adorable. "Oh! You're talking to your Barbies again! What are they saying to you?" I repeatedly tried to explain that I was not talking *to* them, I was talking *for* them, and they were saying some very sexually adventurous things, to say the least. Regular Barbie was upstairs in the den right now tasting the forbidden fruit of Wonder Woman, while old-timey Barbie fetched some clean towels to cover the cream-colored sofa. It wasn't called the Barbie Dream House for nothing!

Soon after giving me the little red sex book to read, my mother decided that it would be okay to bring all of her pornographic material out of exile and pop it back on the bookshelf where it belonged, beside the Boz Scaggs records and dog-eared copy of *Silent Spring*. Movies, toys, magazines—all of them in plain sight—and we took it all in as casually as one might read the Sunday paper. When I discovered a cache of pseudo-Victorian erotica, my dolls started to reference their body parts as "cunnys" and "quivering quims." I thought it was hilarious and figured that my wealth of perverse knowledge would continue to make me a very desirable playmate.

After a while, none of my friends wanted to play dolls with me anymore. I can't really blame them. My expertise had begun to wear on them. It was too much information for them to handle, and too boring for me to have to explain everything over and over again. All of my girlfriends were too preoccupied with Barbie's ever-changing hairstyles to worry that she wasn't getting enough in child support payments, or that she had a fender bender with a handsome new neighbor that she was going to invite over later for a snort.

At the time, their indifference barely registered with me. I was very caught up in these dirty games and didn't have time to waste on my friends' dolls' babyish backstories. My dolls had rich social lives and theirs were bona fide squares—teachers, doctors, vets. Talk to me when your Barbie can work a double shift at the casino, hitchhike home because her car's in the shop, throw together a quick tray of hot Vienna sausages for her friends, and have lesbian sex while her hair sets in rollers for the impromptu block party she's hosting in the back room of the hair salon that night. *Then* maybe we can play.

My mother and her boyfriend would host dinner parties, and at the end of the meal, everyone would just retire to the living room to watch a classic porno instead of a regular movie. There would be popcorn and Rice Krispies squares and lots of convivial conversation. No one was sitting there staring at the television like a pervert in a raincoat at the XXX theater. It was just a bunch of hip adults having a laugh and watching people bang each other. If I happened to come home in the middle of a movie, I would just join the gang and watch along with everyone else. Sometimes things required a little explaining. Most times not.

But my father and my stepmother held staunchly to their belief that children needed to be children; the less information, the better. Their knuckles were white from clinging to the idea of fostering an idyllic childhood. I'm not really sure where it came from, since neither one of them had enjoyed the kind of picture-perfect upbringing that needed to be cryogenically frozen and cloned for the enjoyment of all.

But it was sweet. Leaving packages from Santa until I was well into my twenties. Refusing to swear in front of me until I was almost forty. It still makes my father sputter like a rusty lawn sprinkler when I drop an F-bomb on him.

So when my dad and stepmother tried to have The Talk with me during Bob and Donna's ill-fated honeymoon, I wanted to tell them that I was already familiar with plain old boring lesbianism. I really did. But I just couldn't. I didn't want to take away their *big moment*. Even at that early age, I understood that part of forging a healthy relationship with people you don't see all the time sometimes involves asking questions that you don't really need the answers to and letting someone think they are helping you when you don't really need their help at all.

I also wanted to tell Donna and Bob that I got it. We were interlopers. I wanted to apologize for not getting our *own* hotel room to defile with our wet socks and morose expressions and joyless Deney Terrio *Dance Fever* routines. I was sorry we were getting in the way of their conjugal privileges, too.

But after so many rainy days of observation, I was starting to doubt that they were up to the task as a couple anyway. Having watched so much pornography at an impressionable young age, I had naturally begun to equate sexual prowess with having a great tan, and Bob *was* pretty pale. Donna was no vixen either; she barely ever wore white high-heeled shoes around the motel room, and she wasn't much of a hostess either. I mean, what was up with all the sour faces? And she hardly ever bought enough Hawaiian Punch or squeeze cheese to satisfy the gnawing hunger in our growing bellies.

In *my* play world, the drinks were fresh and free-flowing, the rumaki were hot, and the swingers were all passably attractive. I was beginning to suspect that things weren't necessarily the same in real life. But why expose a nine-year-old to *that* kind of a downer? Let *children* be *children*, for God's sake. There's no need to be cruel about it.

bad kid

Not liking hot ham doesn't make a person a freak. In my opinion, it makes a person seem sensible and capable of discernment. But in my family, consumption of ham equals normal. And deciding whether or not to bite into a big, hot, squeaky Easter ham covered in sweet fruit goo is the barometer that determines whether you are thinking clearly or in one of your "crazy" phases.

"Are you eating ham these days? You're not a vegetarian right now, are you? We're having ham, is that going to be okay, or do I need to make you one of your special 'vegetable stacks'? How many pieces of ham do you want? Have some more ham—there's lots! This one came special ordered from Virginia and weighs twenty-seven pounds! There's even ham in the dessert!"

For the record, I have always disliked hot ham; spearing it with a giant meat fork and slamming it onto a platter reminds me too much of what John the Baptist's head might have looked like, and I find it repulsive. I am, however, still able to enjoy finely diced ham products, and sometimes even thinly sliced cold ham, but only when *I* decide that I am in the mood for it. I am a very mysterious person, I guess, with a lot of complexities.

I can't really blame my parents for their inability to pin me down, or their endless drive to do so. I put them through a lot. I was a scary teenager. A very scary one, in fact, whose multifaceted awfulness soured parental relations well into my twenties, and whose indiscretions are still occasionally brought up to punish me now that I am in my forties. When my parents emerged from my teen years, the scars ran deep and I was forever tragically stamped with the reputation that I am hard to handle and as changeable as a summer breeze. Every assertion I make is still viewed with a kind of bemused suspicion. I somehow warped my parents to the degree that they literally can't believe that I am a good parent, that my husband loves me, or that I don't have some kind of sex dungeon in my house with a bunch of dried-up scrotums hanging on the wall.

And I don't just mean that I was a bad teenager in the usual way. I mean, I *was* horrible in the usual way, of course, but I was *even worse* in a different way. And my parents never knew a thing about it. They should have been much more scared than they actually were.

So years later, when the ultrasound technician told me that I was having a girl, I burst into tears at the thought of what she was going to put me through—because truthfully, I deserve all the emotional pain that is coming to me. I ruined my parents forever. As they read this, they are mirthlessly laughing, and mentally high-fiving each other.

Hitting puberty excavated a wellspring of evil energy in me that led me to the discovery that my parents were vulnerable and had made mistakes that could be exploited in an interesting way. Hating them with the white-hot wrath of a middle-class teenager was a full-time job that I took very seriously. But at least when I was solely occupied with giving my parents stress-related ulcers, I had a sense of self-preservation about me—a shrewdness.

Thank goodness that prior to all this, in a moment of inspiration, my mother had imposed a curfew that I blindly adhered to, at least for a short but vitally important period of time. It preserved my personal safety on a number of occasions. Only a few short months before my transformation into a bitch-on-wheels, I was as innocent as a lamb to the slaughter. And all those times I cheated a horrible outcome just by the skin of my teeth were crystallized in an instant many years later at that ultrasound appointment, as the technician located the girl parts that would mean that I, too, would never sleep comfortably again.

I'm speaking of a simpler time, when I was sweet and soft and doughy and impressionable, and I would eat my parents' ham because I loved them and they had put a lot of effort into the meal and I didn't want to hurt their feelings. In short, I was stupid. That's what fills me with genuine fear as a parent. I'm pretty sure I can handle mean, but I don't quite know how to deal with stupid. When I think back to all the times I engaged in risky behavior and never gave it a second thought, it makes me sick to my stomach imagining my children doing the same kinds of things.

Like most teenagers, I worked desperately to look older than my years, to cultivate the impression that I was willing and available, though the implications of that meant nothing to me. My girlfriends and I were obsessed with projecting the right kind of rocker image, and that meant lots of tight jeans, frosted eyeliner, and a chronic aversion to cold weather outerwear, no matter the subfreezing temperature. Being totally oblivious to winter weather was somehow considered de rigueur in our crowd. In a brave albeit dumb rebuke of fashion trends for no discernible reason at all, I would have worn my leather jacket open at the summit of Mount Everest if I thought there was a chance that a single, homely, male ninth-grader from De La Salle Academy might have been up there looking for a worthy partner to share one of his oxygen canisters with.

I had braces and a feathered haircut, though it never feathered properly, and I was forced to flip the front sides of it with a curling iron. Only the front though. Who cared what the back looked like? *I* couldn't see it anyway, so I figured no one else could either. We dangled decorative roach clips from our hair and purses to signify our extreme coolness, but we just thought they were fun barrettes.

We would sit around Vanessa's basement, listening to Rolling Stones records and weeping our eyes out at all the

sad songs. We still watched *The Uncle Bobby Show* at lunch-
time, played poker for gingersnaps, and dressed up unironi-
cally at Halloween to go trick-or-treating. We constantly
debated who had the better chest, Jon Bon Jovi or David Lee
Roth. Personally, I found Jon Bon Jovi too feminine and
slender—translation: gay. I was a mad David Lee Roth girl; I
loved his hairy chest, but wasn't entirely sure why. I knew I
wanted to rub my face in it, but that was about it. I also suffered from a relentless desire to have either Hall or Oates
sing a duet with me, it didn't really matter which one. Although in my fantasy life, all we did was hold hands afterward, while they complimented me on my natural ability and
effortless recall of the words to "One on One."

Despite my tarted-up exterior, I had never been kissed,
had never come close to being on a date, and had never in a
million years considered having a boy go up my shirt or anywhere else for that matter. I was familiar with all things
sexual but had no desire to drink from that particular cup.
So when I met Dan from Buffalo, I was oblivious to his
intentions.

We were sitting near each other at the Police Picnic, one
of those open-air concerts with multiple bands on the bill.
My girlfriends and I liked to see live music and had been to
several concerts, though we never partook in any of the
antics. We didn't drink or smoke pot, but we liked to go to
heavy-metal shows and stand quietly in the nosebleeds, too
self-conscious to sway or appear to enjoy the music in any
way. Occasionally, we would raise our devil horns, but only

if everyone else around us had done it first, and we only ever knew the bands' number one hits. Sometimes we would see a groupie go by, or someone who looked appealingly slutty, and we would jealously contemplate her tight satin pants and well-feathered hair, feeling shabby in our stupid tight *jeans* with our stupid *poorly* feathered hair.

Dan was tall and tan, with a big shock of tightly curled blond hair and a wide white smile. I think he was interested in my girlfriend, but when she, paralyzed with fear, was unable to respond to his questions, he moved down the line and eventually got to me. I would do. I was sort of witty, and more "worldly" than my friends—though that's not really saying much, since they were first-generation Canadians, and their hardworking Polish parents barely spoke English and wouldn't pay for cable. It was difficult having to hold their hands through the particulars of the *Falcon Crest* family lineage, but I was a very giving person.

There is no way I could have come across as any older than thirteen. I still had braces on my teeth, for God's sake. I was thirteen, but I probably looked eight, though I definitely claimed to be in my twenties and in college. Dan and all his friends certainly were. They had probably graduated many years earlier, in fact. When I told him my major was geography, I was unable to elaborate any further and had no reason to believe that anyone studying geography in college would ever need to elaborate. I mean, wasn't it obvious? I was studying where all the countries in the world were, coloring in each one with a different shade of pencil crayon. It's possible that I could have pointed to the Middle East on a map if asked, but just barely.

After the most shallow conversation imaginable between an adult and a child pretending to be an adult, he invited me back to his hotel room for a pizza party. Even his friends looked horrified, and they were his wingmen. I wanted to go so badly. I could just taste all that hot, delicious pizza and imagine all the deep adult conversation I would be having in the good company of a handsome man from south of the border in his lonely hotel room. The promise of passing for an adult was too good to resist; plus, he had a car, which was so far out of my league that it was as if he had offered to fly me back to the Sheraton Hotel on the wings of Falkor from *The Neverending Story*, which happened to be my favorite movie at the time . . . because I was a little girl.

My friends said no to the tantalizing invitation, which made it impossible for me to accept. We whisper-fought in front of Dan and his friends for twenty minutes, through the entire encore. They weren't upset that a grown man was transparently trying to seduce a gaggle of thirteen-year-olds, because my friends were just as excited as I was about the prospect of eating pizza that we didn't have to pay for. They were simply concerned that we would get in trouble if we didn't make it home by curfew. As a mature college student in the field of "World Geography," I would have difficulty explaining that my parents had imposed something as "retardenated" as a curfew, but fortunately, I was very quick on my feet.

"I can't. My mother was hit by a carpet-cleaning van."

"Oh, I'm so sorry! That's awful—is she okay?"

She actually *had* recently been bumped by a carpet-cleaning van at a crosswalk, but all that had materialized was a huge bruise on her hip and the beginnings of an angry letter-writing campaign to the municipal authorities regarding pedestrian safety.

"No. Not at all. She's in a coma. She needs us to come home and check on all her tubes." I had also recently seen *The Other Side of the Mountain* again on TV, so I was something of an expert on medical interventions.

"Why is she at home? Shouldn't she be in a hospital?"

"She doesn't want people to feel sorry for her. *I think the hardest time for her is waking up in the morning . . . those moments before she remembers who she is, and thinks instead about who she was.*"

I prayed that it hadn't been his favorite "triumph of the human spirit" movie, too, but then he offered me a ride home anyway. I was actually supposed to sleep over at my girl-friend's house, but I didn't want him to know that because I thought only kids had slumber parties and it might give away my real age. And although technically I was staying over at a friend's house, I still respected my mother's curfew. I worried about the possibility that she was "all-seeing" and would somehow find out, and bar me from attending the kinds of grown-up events at which adult men would try to lure me back to their hotel rooms.

"No. My mother would get really upset if someone drove me all the way home."

"Wouldn't it be faster than taking the subway and then a bus this late at night?" I struggled with that one.

"Yeah, but she doesn't like me taking the easy way out. She wants me to know about hardship and the value of a dollar and how far a dollar can take you on public transportation. And she likes to see my transfers from all my subway trips when I get home. It reminds her of how great it is to be able to travel on the subways since she can't do it anymore herself."

"I thought she was in a coma."

"Definitely. I usually just sit by the side of her bed and show her all my transfers and she just tries to blink out the words 'I love you.' It's really sad." I looked sad all right, but only because I wasn't going to a stranger's hotel in the middle of nowhere for late-night snacks.

It wouldn't be the last time my mother's decision to impose curfew would intervene on my behalf. My girlfriend and I used to go to the summer carnival every year and hang around in front of the ride that went backward in a loop and played obnoxiously loud music and sirens. I think it was called the Polar Express, so named for all the Eskimos airbrushed on the walls in the tunnel portion of the loop. It was the kind of ride that would make anyone over the age of seventeen throw up in a trash can immediately upon disembarking, but for some reason, it was adored by all teenagers.

The ride was notorious for being a pickup spot. Everyone would stand around dumbly pretending not to look at one another, while they secretly scoped everyone out. No one ever seemed to actually go on the ride; nobody could have afforded the cost of all the tickets it would have taken to actually *enjoy* the ride over and over again. And anyway, who would want to take the chance of messing up their long, badly curled, rocker side locks?

Vanessa and I were no exception to that rule. We stood there night after night. When we got into the amusement park, it was the first place we went, the only place we stayed for longer than three minutes, and the last place on our agenda for the whole night. We closed the park every night we were there, on that very spot, like so many others with us and before us. We didn't talk to any of the people there, and they never really talked to us, though we saw them almost every day for the two weeks that the amusement park was open.

It wasn't really clear what we were after. We were repulsed by the majority of the boys who were standing there with us, and were threatened by the girls who looked better than us. If anyone approached us, we gave them the cold shoulder and rebuffed them almost immediately . . . until one night, when Vanessa suddenly erupted with puberty and I didn't. Her interest was piqued by two older-looking guys whom we had never seen before. They walked up to us, and as I steadied myself to coolly reject them in the usual way, I found Vanessa strangely enjoying their company. They were in their twenties, unemployed, and looking to party with two sexy single ladies such as ourselves. Never mind that we were thirteen and a half.

One of them looked like he had been the weaker, slightly withered conjoined twin of the other, successfully separated by surgeons but doomed to forever live in his handsome, healthy brother's shadow. He looked like the smaller, uglier, slightly albino version of his friend, with less of everything, including normal pigmentation. Naturally, I got *him*. Even if I had been interested in anything sex-related, it wouldn't have occurred to me to have it with him.

Vanessa and her handsome paramour began the clumsy dance of the Polar Express courtship, while I stuck it out with his albatross of a friend. *She* was the one pretending to be in college now, and she needed my support. By my estimation, she was doing a terrible job of faking her age; she put no effort into it whatsoever, and mostly just stood there awkwardly with him, not saying much of anything. The silence would have been deafening had it not been for the screaming sound track of the Polar Express filling the void in the background. As a good friend, I felt it was incumbent upon me to take the ball and run with it. I used the opportunity to present myself as a student of child psychology, specializing in child abuse.

I detailed a particular case that was on my mind. A young African-American girl from a low-income, single-parent family was being subjected to a series of physical abuses, and no one had been willing to intervene on her behalf so far. What was our responsibility as a society? The police weren't interested, her teachers weren't getting involved, even her own *doctor* had ignored the warnings of her benevolent neighbors, the Evans family. This girl—let's call her "Penny"—had been burned *with an iron,* at the hands of her own *mother,* for God's sake.

As I chronicled the entire story line from my favorite *"very special* two-part episode" of *Good Times,* the men could not have paid me less attention. Having determined that I, an annoying smidge of a girl, could somehow hinder their plan for us with my constant chatter, they chose to ignore me and put the full-court press on Vanessa.

Soon after, we were invited to their borrowed downtown condo for pizza. I'm not sure what it was about us that continually suggested that we were in need of free pizza, but there it was again, the Magic Word. But, oh no—we had this curfew we were supposed to comply with, how awful! To have the chance for free pizza and not be able to take it! Was this going to be the way things always were for us? Missed opportunity after missed opportunity?

No, sir, not this time. We were happy to jump in their car and head over to their apartment in a dangerous part of town, with one caveat: this was definitely going to have to be the kind of pizza that you could order and receive in under thirty minutes, and then we would have to go and they couldn't give us any "guff" about it.

As soon as we got to their generically furnished apartment, they offered us Valium, which we both took. I had no idea what Valium was, but in retrospect, I'm glad I took it because it probably dulled my senses enough for me not to panic at the situation we had placed ourselves in for the simple love of food. Plenty of Valium and now liquor was on offer, but no pizza appeared to be forthcoming, and I started to get antsy about it.

I tried to plant a seed of doubt in Vanessa's head about leaving. We weren't getting what we came for, and it was getting to the time when we would really have to hustle if we were going to make our curfew. I was really pissed and starting to feel uncomfortable about being watched over by two grown men. Who were really, *really* watching us . . . or rather, I presume, waiting for us to pass out so they could have sex with our lifeless bodies. Fortunately for someone of my size, I have an exceptionally high tolerance for pharmaceutical drugs. I'm like a horse that way. If you're going to give me drugs and you expect something interesting to happen, then you better really dose me. You better get in it to win it, or your so-called drugs are just going to wake me up and make me feel refreshed.

At any rate, I had more important things on my mind at the time. I was so fixated on the idea of pizza that you'd have thought I'd just had my jaws unwired after six months of liquids-only nourishment. They *claimed* to have ordered it on the phone in the other room, but I was starting to get suspicious. Wouldn't they have checked with us to see what kind of toppings we wanted first? How rude. What if they had ordered it with pineapple or olives? It would take so much time for me to pick off the gross toppings, the whole endeavor hardly seemed worth it.

There was some talk about "not letting us go," which, thanks to the miracle of Valium, I was able to ignore completely, taking for granted that we would be able to leave whenever we wanted. For all of the random fears that ruled my life—the fear of Lizzie Borden's ghost, the fear of gypsy curses, the fear of being impregnated by an alien—nowhere in my tortured psyche was there anything about being assaulted in an apartment by two strange men who had fed me drugs. Which actually seemed to be imminent (though I hadn't really noticed that part yet, and I didn't even really think about it until years later). I didn't know where I was, couldn't see a phone anywhere in the apartment, and had no money in my wallet for a taxi. I also didn't know that I was the only one who actually *wanted* to leave. Vanessa was having a good time with those two duds and she didn't want to go. I begged her and begged her, but she refused. They eventually let me leave, I guess because not only had I become a seriously annoying liability but my friend had stayed on to party without me.

I made it home on time, put on my flannel *Little House on the Prairie*–style nightgown, and settled in for a night of virginity and being thirteen years old. I found out the next day that Vanessa was officially dating both guys at the same time, and from that point forward I could never look at her face without picturing it in the throes of an orgasm. It was hard to go back to gingersnap poker after that.

Shortly thereafter, I met a much older man on the bus that I took home from ninth grade every day. His name was Alan, and he looked a lot like Dan, only his shoes were shabbier and he smelled like patchouli. I'm going to put his age at thirty. He lived in a basement apartment a few streets north of me, and I know that because I went there one day, just because he asked me to and I felt weird about saying no.

Alan had struck up a conversation with me because I always carried a flute to school and he was "interested in music." Although my flute case clearly stated the name of my high school in bold stenciled letters, I was able to convince myself that I had convinced *him* that I was a professional musician for the Toronto Symphony Orchestra. He asked me if I would come over to his place and play him something. I agreed, and then spent the next twenty minutes sweating profusely and wondering if my woodwind rendition of "Dancing on the Ceiling" would be enough to convince him that I was for real. Our ninth-grade orchestra specialized in easy listening and ran the gamut from Lionel Richie up-tempo ballads to the classic-rock stylings of Bread.

The walls of his apartment were crowded with roughly hewn shelving units, each crammed with pickle jars and canned peaches and spilling over with baskets of onions and potatoes. But the place did not look lived in. There were no bare walls upon which to affix any posters, there wasn't much furniture to speak of, and it was cold . . . I guess to keep the vegetables fresh. Were it not for the untidy captain's bed jammed in the corner, he could have been a mature street urchin living in some family's basement unbeknownst to them.

What kind of grown man still slept in a captain's bed anyway? Weren't you just supposed to hide your *Mad* magazines and your masturbation glove (worn to prevent hair from developing on your palms) in it? Given the bountiful harvest lining the shelves, he was probably storing turnips and carrots in all the drawers. He didn't seem to have any kind of kitchen in which to boil and sterilize the mason jars for all of his summer preserves either. I hadn't asked him what he did for a living, and by the looks of things, I guessed the answer was probably going to be "not much." My stow-away theory was becoming more and more likely. But I didn't have time to worry that he lived in some old lady's root cellar; I was far too busy worrying that my performance would not be impressive enough to sustain the illusion that *I* had so carefully crafted.

He offered me all kinds of drugs and poppers, liquors and "smokables," which I refused on the basis of musicianship. We sat on the floor, since he clearly couldn't afford a sofa or chair, and he rubbed my shoulders as I awkwardly tried to piece together my crappy borrowed instrument with the flair of a professional. Numb with fear of failure, I barely registered his thirty-year-old hands sliding all over my back in an attempt to be seductive and irresistible. Citing embouchure exhaustion from my extra-long professional practices, I hacksawed my way through "Pachelbel's Canon," while he tried to mesmerize me with his sensuous caresses.

That messy captain's bed started looming large on the other side of the room, and I grew increasingly nervous about his insistence on helping me achieve a relaxed state. It was starting to dawn on me that I should reconsider my willingness to accompany strange men to their love caves when I had no intention of surrendering myself to them. For the first time, perhaps, I was starting to feel a bit under siege. Was there a possibility that he *hadn't* been interested in hearing me play? That his "love of music" had just been some kind of crazy ploy to get me to come over to his apartment?

I shook it off. *No one* would make something like that up just to get someone interested in them. That would be wrong.

I began to focus on getting myself out of there without being too insulting to my host. After all, I *had* willingly followed him home after meeting him on a public bus, so in a sense I had accepted his hospitality, and as such, owed him some civility. Failing that, my plan basically involved defecating on myself.

I had heard a story about how to protect oneself against the unwanted advances of men. If someone is trying to get at you, the scenario goes, your best strategy for extricating yourself from the situation is to act as crazy as possible. You should shout things like "I have herpes!" and "I'm warning you, I love to bite penises in half!" and bark like a dog—basically, whatever it takes to scare off your potential attacker.

The nuclear option was to poop your own pants. Nobody messes with a girl who is willing to poop her own pants. I didn't feel like things were quite progressing to *that* level, but I readied myself to pee in a circle on his floor and began making excuses as to why a mature, professional musician such as myself had to get home for dinner with my mom.

"I have to be home at five on the dot or my mother will freak."

"Well, you're pretty close by, can't you just stay a little longer and then I'll walk you home? Can't your mother do without you for one dinner?"

"No. She really needs me. I take care of her. I have to feed her, and by five o'clock she's really hungry. I can't let her feed herself. She can't."

"Why?"

"She was born without arms. She's a human worm."

I had recently seen a short film in my social studies class about a woman with no arms. She lived a normal life and was able to do all these miraculous things, like drive a specially rigged car and care for her babies with her long toes. She would wear clogs when she went grocery shopping, and when she needed to check a cantaloupe for ripeness, she would just slip off one of her clogs, give the melon a squeeze, and slip it into her grocery cart. Some people in the grocery store found it appalling, but I was very high-minded and knew that she was just being proactive and handi-*capable*. By the look on Alan's face when I brought up my human-worm mom, I could tell that he was narrow-minded and probably the kind of person who, unlike me, would never buy three-way lightbulbs from the adult assisted-living facility in town.

"She's not a *freak*, you know. She's a very proud person. She can change a diaper with her feet."

"Then why can't she feed herself?"

"She *can*, she just doesn't like to. She likes me to roll her gurney out to the patio, and then we eat dinner together at five and enjoy the quiet."

"Why is she on a gurney? She has legs, doesn't she?"

I didn't appreciate Alan's interrogation tactics. I just wanted to get the hell out of there with minimal effort, but this was really turning into a tour de force. "Well, obviously she's trying to preserve her feet, because she needs them to be soft and pliable for when she really needs them—to brush her hair or open a jar or something—like a hand model who has to wear rubber gloves all the time to minimize wear and tear."

I was on my way up the stairs and out of the basement, and just kept going with it. "She used to have a helper ferret, but then he was strangled by the cord from our venetian blinds. You're supposed to keep them up high so that babies don't get tangled up in them, but there aren't any safeguarding instructions for having a polecat ferret in the house. He was able to climb up the cord, and I guess he just got excited and then couldn't unwind himself or something . . . I don't think he suffered. He had a very peaceful look on his face when she found him . . ."

Unaware that I had now, in fact, figuratively "pooped my pants," I congratulated myself profusely on my gifted story-telling abilities and hightailed it home. As disappointed as Alan probably was to have let such an obvious virgin and stupid person leave his grandma's basement with her lady-flower intact, he had to have known on some level that it wouldn't have been worth it.

Shortly thereafter, I adopted a brand-new attitude with respect to older gentlemen, known as, *"Fuck you, you fucking pervert. I'm fucking fourteen years old!"* I don't really know where it came from, this proud spine that thrust upward out of nowhere, but I began putting it to good use. With my refusal to eat hot ham soon to follow.

old lady hands

I can't remember her name offhand, but I had a distant aunt who was a butcher at a meat-packing plant. And by "butcher," I don't mean to imply that she was in there gently frenching the remaining flesh from pasture-fed lamb chops. She was employed hauling carcasses and doing the rough cuts on a metal slab in a meat factory. My father called her Rameeda the Beast, and it suited her perfectly. She was about eight feet tall, was missing two fingers, and had a voice that coincidentally recalled the sound of a band saw cutting through human knuckles. The last time I saw her, she was smoking hands-free and microwaving a prime rib roast for Christmas dinner, while the rest of us were busy patting down the dining room chairs with Scotch tape to get rid of the molting fur of an ancient basset hound named Mr. McDiggity.

My aunt's missing fingers haunted me. It looked like she had sewn the ends of her fingers closed with black yarn, and then cauterized them with boiling snake venom. I was mesmerized by them. I don't know if *she* suffered from any form of phantom limb syndrome, but *I* certainly did that Christmas, watching her tiny stumps struggle to attach the paper crowns that were meant to adorn the bony ends of our crown rib roast.

"Aww, fuck it. Merry Christmas, everyone," she said, as she slammed the naked roast onto the table. "Digg-ski in-ski."

I bet her hands caused her a lot of trouble in life, and having some snippy ten-year-old refuse to eat her mashed potatoes because she had dangled one of her finglets in them for a nanosecond one Christmas couldn't have helped. I get that now. I totally get it.

I mean, I may have all ten of my fingers, but none of them are attractive on any level. I have old lady hands; I've always had them. If you look at pictures of me as an infant, you'd think that the hands of a tiny eighty-year-old hooker had been Photoshopped onto my otherwise smooth, alabaster baby body. They're kind of small and wrinkly and chapped, and as I age, they're exploring ever new ways to disappoint me. They're getting spotty and yellowish from sun damage; I have a tiny (what I think might be a) wart on one finger, and now when you pinch the skin, it kind of stands up on its own for a while before settling back to normal. I have a vague recollection of mocking old people for this very feature when I was a young girl, acts of unkindness I now regret.

I think we can all agree that most people *enjoy* getting a massage. It usually feels good when someone else's hands work their way around your tired, aching muscles, even if the person administering the rubdown isn't a professional massage therapist. But when *my* hands are involved, there's an almost instant feeling of disappointment, followed by growing irritation, and ending with my hands being halted mid-rubdown and patted out of pity. My hands are incapable of convincingly sensual touch.

I'm the only person on Earth who can repel someone with a massage. I don't know if it's the pointiness of my fingers or the unsatisfying smallness of the span of my hands that is the problem, but either way, my massages are universally rejected. Judging from people's reactions to them, my massages are about as sexy as sprinkling dry corn on your back and having a pack of chickens peck their way up and down your spine.

My fingernails are so tiny that they weird out manicurists, and I have sweaty palms with a mole on one of them, which my dermatologist assures me will one day probably turn into melanoma and take my life. I bite my nails, I bite my cuticles. If I could somehow bite someone else's hands off and attach them to my wrists, that would actually be great.

It takes a lot of mental energy for me to keep my hands out of the public eye. It's hard to do stuff like pay for things or hold on to a subway pole without revealing my hands to people. Obviously, mitten season is my favorite.

I don't mean to disparage them entirely, because it seems karmically bad to complain about my fully functioning human hands when people like my aunt and Bob Dole have to make do without. I'll give you this—they work much better than a metal hook. And if you were to put my hands on a dog, let's say, that dog would be able to do all kinds of incredible things, like clip its own toenails, and dial 911 if something went wrong.

Hands like these make a statement—a statement like "I clean other people's toilets on a daily basis" or "I gut fish for a living, outside, in frigid weather." Cheerful, "glass half full" people always look at my hands and say, "Oh! You must be an old soul." But I know all they're really saying is, "Wow. Please don't touch my taut, youthful skin with those leathery hand-claws."

Sometimes old people look at me, then they scan down to my hands, and they give me a kind of "what's up" look, like we're the same. It hurts a little at first, of course, but I'll take it. I'm a big enough person to take it and run with it. "Yes! I'm an old soul! Hands never lie!"

In my case, though, it's true. I believe that I actually am an old soul. I *get* old people. I mean, I really get them. And I'm well aware that one day the rest of my body is going to catch up to the train wreck that is my hands. I know exactly what's coming—graying pubes (what's left of them, that is), yellowy eyeballs, footwear worn expressly for the relief of bunions. But I'm not scared. I'm going to be ready for it.

Most people won't be. They think of old age as something that happens to other people, something they'd rather die than experience. And when all those people are busy falling apart, cracking their hips and shaking their fists at noisy teenagers, that's when I'm really going to shine. I'm going to come out on top—the Benevolent Overlord of the Old People! I've been training for it my whole life. I learned from the best.

I was mostly raised by my maternal grandmother, and until the age of seven, by *her* mother as well. I lived with my parents a little bit, and I sort of went back and forth between houses, but there, at the center of my universe, were the double grannies, patching up the cracks in my parents' parenting, packing sensible backup lunches for me, and always being there to wipe my face with a warm wet cloth if I tried going to school again dripping with hair product after an unsuccessful third attempt at a Jheri curl.

And after my great-grandmother died, my grandmother seemed to find her purpose in teaching me everything she knew about being old. Well, to her it was just living, I suppose, but there I was beside her all the time, wide-eyed, absorbing everything. Based on all my grade-school photographs, I was a quick learner. Effectively vetoing my mother's nonstrategy of letting me choose my own outfits for school, my grandmother always had a plan-B outfit at the ready. Whenever possible, my grandmother would intercept me in the hallway at school and switch me into something that looked "smart" and "age appropriate." Well, appropriate to *her* age, anyway.

Early on, she favored the David Niven look: monochromatic turtleneck and slim-leg slack combos, cat-burglar style.

And a photo from my third-grade "concerned guidance counselor" phase shows me sporting a Dorothy Hamill wedge and looking luminous in butter-soft pink leather culottes and panty hose with a pair of dark brown negative heel shoes. (A girl from my class stands behind me in that photo wearing a DON'T TOUCH MY TUTS T-shirt that I secretly coveted, but outwardly, I agreed with my grandmother that it totally made her look like a whore.)

My grandmother would send me to phys ed in a navy-blue, puffy-sleeved, one-piece cashmere sweat suit with a patent-leather belt, and warn me not to sweat in it, since it was dry-clean only. I hadn't broken a sweat so far in my life, so this was a pretty easy directive to follow. I looked fantastic, but I couldn't have hit a softball if there was a gun to the back of my head, so what difference did it make. Anyway, who could have shinnied up a rope with a patent-leather belt on? It would have gotten snagged on things . . . I'm sure . . . if I had ever tried it.

Being cocooned in a sweater-tard was the least of my worries, as I struggled to protect myself from all the balls flying haphazardly around the room. I tried to focus instead on more and more elaborate excuses for why I wasn't able to participate that day and had to sit it out on the bench: scoliosis-based fears, highly secretive and therefore unmentionable lady problems, meningitis. And if the roving AARP fashion photographer had happened to drop by my gym class unannounced, *then* who would have had the last laugh? Us! In your *face*, children in proper athletic wear!

Under the careful tutelage of my grandmother, I learned to listen to the beat of my own fashion drummer. Even at my prom, while all the other girls went for strapless taffeta, I went in a decidedly Bea Arthur direction, eschewing over-all attractiveness and youthful sexuality for a free-flowing cream pantsuit with a matching mid-thigh-length kimono-style jacket. The way it ironed out all those burgeoning female curves and made me look as bland as a plate of Cracker Barrel chicken and dumplings . . . mmm, my date took one look at me and put his erection away for the next six months. But my grandmother and I, celebrating over a glass of Ovaltine, both agreed at the time that I really pulled it off.

We were as close as two people could get.

All of her friends looked up to her. While these old ladies aged gracelessly— all crotchety and falling apart at the seams to the point where catching one "bad wind" could lay them out for a week—my grandmother kept it together physically, and always looked and dressed a little like Rona Barrett, whom she considered to be a real firecracker. She applied makeup well, stayed slim, and never ever wore anything but stylish Italian heels. Even when my mother bought a run-down farmstead and invited her to visit in the dead of winter in the aftermath of a catastrophic ice storm, my grandmother toddled off to visit the barn in a freshly pressed pair of be-dazzled denim slacks with a coordinated Western-style chambray vest, an angora cowl-neck sweater, a winter-white wool car coat, and a cashmere accessories set: shell pink gloves with a matching tam perched at a jaunty angle on top of her head.

She was hardwired to care about her appearance even as she was overtaken by a pack of unruly goats. Through the kitchen window, I saw them take her down and rip the tam from her head. As they dragged their dirty goat beards across her face and trampled her fine winter coat, she did a quick under-eye sweep to make sure her mascara wasn't running. Not that she was superficial; she just had a terrific understanding of the power of her own image. She realized that if she let herself go in old age, no one would ever rush over to serve her at the fish counter, doctors wouldn't listen to her— she would disappear. And she was not going out like that.

If you were of her generation and you were a man, you could practically do anything and your behavior would be excused. My great-grandmother had married a man who used to grab at women's breasts and vaginas as they walked by, and everyone would just chuckle, "Oh, *him*? He's harmless. He's just a dirty old man." And then they would quietly gather up the girl children and usher them into the other room, away from him.

It was disgusting. But there he was—a sex pervert at large, free to grab crotches as if he were just helping himself to another serving from a passing dim sum cart. If you were a woman, though, and you did something as seemingly innocuous as letting your hair go gray, it was over. You might as well live on a park bench and layer yourself with old pizza boxes for warmth.

My grandmother got that. Here was a woman who took my mother to get her first perm and dye job when she was *three years old*. It was unthinkable for her to have given birth to a child who didn't have short, curly blond hair and blue eyes, like Shirley Temple. Even though she herself (and my grandfather, for that matter) had straight dark brown hair and brown eyes, she was shattered when my mother emerged with a shock of dark hair and didn't immediately burst into a rendition of "On the Good Ship Lollipop" worthy of a record deal.

I don't recognize my mother from a single photograph taken of her as a child. There is simply no correlation between those photographs and what nature had intended for her. I, of course, find this hilarious. But my mother does not. She has terrible memories of my grandmother eventually giving up on her dream of producing a blond cherub and taking her to the hair salon for something called "The Italian Boy." I told her that, based on all the photos I've seen, she made a *very* handsome little Italian boy. She finds this most hilarious.

Meanwhile, my grandmother thought my mother's gay male friends were just fashionable straight guys with toned muscles and really tidy roommates. She did those low-impact Jack LaLanne exercise moves and they *actually* kept her fit. I'd come into the living room and she'd be in front of the TV, gently moving in a skirt and blouse with a pair of Isotoner footies on for traction. If I asked her a question, she'd stop me and say, "Ask me when I'm finished doing my leggies."

Leg lifts were "leggies," any arm-related exercises were obviously "armies," and her minimally invasive floor exercises were known as "poochies," to help get rid of her pooch.

Our favorite game to play together was Do You Wish I Was Fat Like That? We would go to the mall and people-watch in between munching carrot muffins and browsing for matching sale-priced Liz Claiborne fashions. Every once in a while we would end up following someone with a big ass and my grandmother would sigh and say, "Do I look like that?" Then she would ask disingenuously, "Do you wish I was fat like that? Wouldn't I be more fun? Wouldn't I seem more jolly?"

My job was to assure her that she was perfect just as she was. And that's really how I felt. No matter what, we always spoke honestly with each other and enjoyed each other's company. Even when I was at my worst as a teen, she could instantly bring me back to civility with a couple of thawed-out chicken kievs and a *Newhart/Cagney & Lacey* twofer.

When I did my first play, she blubbered incessantly with pride from the moment she entered the building until three days later, when she was still barely able to compose herself. My acting career became her obsession. We would watch shows together and she would wonder why I wasn't in any of them. Then she would ask with a sigh, "Do you want me to go down to the station and put your name in?" as though that were the key; you just had to express an interest in being a star and that was all they needed to know to get you started on the road to success.

My grandmother greatly admired celebrities and people of a certain pedigree, but only if they were American. She adored the Kennedys, worshipped the Reagans, wished she were Doris Day; she would have done anything to have been born in the States and be able to claim them as her own people. Having summered in the United States for much of her childhood, she was convinced that she had basically been born there, and as such, adopted a slight difficult-to-place accent whenever she thought someone was picking on America. The more you noticed it, the worse it got, until her defense of Oliver North and his involvement in the Iran-Contra affair was distilled down to the words *"Leave us alone! Weah ahr Ahmahricahns!"*

Her obsession with American celebrities ran so deep that she practically refused to admit they had been born vaginally. She insisted that they had simply emerged, glowing and smooth from their gossamer star nests, surviving by gently nibbling on the most tender leaves and shoots of spring; their twenty-four-inch-waisted bodies permanently draped in the spangly creations of Bob Mackie; the only discharge their tiny bodies could ever emit was in the form of a fragrant potpourri of organic matter that would make your tomatoes come in bigger than ever, should you ever be privileged enough to have one of them over for a garden party.

She respected television and its glittering denizens so much that she *couldn't* not watch it, even when she hated it. She disliked certain shows with such intensity that she watched them every day just to spite them and punish them.

Trying to effect change on *Knots Landing* with tongue clicks and exasperated sighs was one thing, but her whole body got involved when *The Young and the Restless* came on.

With an alarming level of passion she would shriek at the television, "*Damn* you, *Victor Newman. Damn* you. Argh! Oh, I could just *smash* him." And sometimes when he spoke she would have to run in and out of the room, listening to the scenes without looking at him. She got so worked up by the sight of his bushy mustache that her hands would clench and her jaw would tighten; I later came to recognize that as Gam-lust. She literally found him irresistible, and it made her so angry with herself that she wanted to put her fist through a window. (I am similarly conflicted by my fascination with CBS News correspondent Lara Logan, but in my case, it doesn't make me want to shatter glass. It just makes me want to sniff her pretty hair. I imagine it smells like freshly picked Honey Crisp apples.)

Transitioning into an oldie can be a scary experience, I think. Will it go as smoothly for you as it will for me? Probably not, but one can dream. Who knows, perhaps one day, one of you may even be called up to the position of *Deputy* Benevolent Overlord of the Old People! (Of course, don't get your hopes up. I may be old at heart, but that doesn't mean I don't have high standards that you are probably incapable of living up to.)

Since I've been steeped in Granny juice for as long as I can remember, insight into the old lady brain comes very naturally to me, and I think I can help you out. Recently, I attended a big luncheon and sat at the same table as a woman from the Kennedy family. I was feeling very uncomfortable and out of place, so I started making eyes at the little old lady beside me, since all she had to do was look at my hands and know that I was going to be *simpatico*. The only thing she really talked to me about was the Kennedy woman's chest, and her shocking lack of "boobies." The little old lady was disgusted. "Couldn't she have at least bothered to put on a pair of *falsies* before coming out to lunch? These young women today. Slovenly."

These are the sorts of attitudes that you are going to need to be able to identify and adopt as your own. They may seem foreign to you at first, but give them time. Soon enough they will start to metastasize inside your elder brain, and all of it will make sense. Right around the time you start thinking that teddy bears in Scottish tams *actually are* cute after all, and that they would make a great stocking stuffer for your fifteen-year-old niece. There are do's and don'ts, of course. But in the spirit of growing old gracefully, feel free to peruse the suggestions I have arrived at, after years of experience, and accept all of them.

1. First things first. Know for sure that wearing shorts or inappropriate footwear too early in the spring, when it's not really that warm yet, will give you "the rheumatism." I often find myself shaking my head sadly at people who have jumped the gun on the season and have cast aside their pants when the nights are still cool. Something is going to happen to their legs in about fifty-odd years—I don't know what exactly, but I do know it will be terrible for these Young Turks!

2. Also, you're going to want to pick up "sad head shaking" as soon as possible. It will form the core of your elderly response mechanism, and should not be overlooked.

3. And don't forget to liberally sprinkle the word *the* wherever possible. Why have high blood pressure when you could have The High Blood Pressure. It makes everything in your life sound about twice as potentially lethal and, therefore, dicey and thrilling. Like tangling with an alligator, or lifting the toilet seat lid and finding a funnel-web spider lying in wait.

4. Don't wear cheap plastic shoes. They will give you corns. What are corns, you may ask? Well, *don't* ask, because if you have never seen one, you will not believe that they are possible. But they are, and if you get one, you will definitely know it and no one will want to be near your feet ever again. *Corn*. In your *feet*. You better recognize.

5. As a vulnerable old wrinkle pup, doing the things that you used to do all the time, like drinking a cold drink while eating warm cake or brownies hot out of the oven, can kill you. Many other seemingly innocuous things can kill you as well. Cold drafts on your neck in movie theaters. Crisp-tender vegetables. Retrieving voice mail messages or Going on The Yahoo. Take a toque wherever you go, and don't try to operate any machinery of any kind without a grandchild present.

6. If you're going to have young people over, sitting on the couch in their shorts, you are definitely going to want to put a beach towel down. Otherwise, their youthful bodily oils are going to be absorbed by the fabric and leave a giant

greasy patch where their bodies once were, and that is repulsive. I mean, it's not going to happen right away or anything, but I think they'd be pleasantly surprised to find out how filthy they are. Make sure they know this.

7. Although it's technically okay to do it *sometimes,* you shouldn't rewind your cassette tapes to your favorite song too often or you will wear them out, and then you will have to buy new ones. It's best just to listen to every other song on one side of the tape, flip it over, give the other side a listen, and then flip it back to the side that has your favorite song. Eventually, you'll find your way back to the one you like, and you should really try to drink it in; it's going to be a while before you hear it again.

8. Frowning causes wrinkles, and so does pushing your face into your pillow while you sleep. Even if you are wearing painful plastic curlers to set your hair, try to sleep on your back anyway, like a pharaoh in a sarcophagus, or all that face mushing will age you prematurely. Also, remember to put Scotch tape across your forehead while you sleep, so that you don't frown when you are having nightmares. Which you *will* be having because of the hard plastic curlers embedding themselves in your scalp. Don't worry, it's definitely worth it. Maybe.

9. Eat an apple every day. They're good for you and they also brush your teeth! (Sort of.)

10. Also, brush your teeth.

11. Cosmetic plastic surgery is weird. Do not do it unless you are Wayne Newton.

12. A girdle is a must. How else are you planning to whittle your waist down to the twenty-four-inch mark? What's that, you say? That's physically impossible? That's unhealthy? Quit being such a pussy and get on it. Deep breathing and the ability to eat more than one Tic Tac at a time for your lunch are overrated.

13. Showers are like having water *attack you*. Civilized people take baths.

14. When entertaining, hot dogs are *not* the same thing as sausages. Hot dogs are made of cow lips and cow vaginas, along with a lot of other crazy shit. Sausages are savory and delicious; they are also possibly made with lips and vaginas, but are more distinctive tasting, so they're better. Especially the German kind. Prick them with a fork before you try to cook them, otherwise they might swell up and fly off the barbecue, like they did at my First Communion. An elderly person would be ill-advised to risk this sort of catastrophe, as they are not fast enough to outrun the ensuing barrage of molten hot bratwurst. Don't even get me started on corn on the cob. I'm just saying.

15. Wear a bra, but not at night, so that your aging bodily fluids can sluggishly redistribute themselves. You can also take it off for your gentle bath, but then put it right back on. If you have anything in the way of boobies and don't adhere to these two rules, your lady lumps will end up looking like two heavy boccie balls dangling from your chest in a pair of tube socks.

16. Also, full-seated panties are a must. Many people call them "granny panties"—this is inappropriate and disparag-

ing. Think of them as a clean, absorbent cotton insurance policy against what is going to happen to you in the future should you happen to laugh and sneeze at the same time. At some point, your thong strap is going to disappear into the folds of your buttocks, and this is counterintuitive to the thong's original purpose, which is to say, sexiness. Embrace a broad cotton gusset and get on with your life.

17. Finally, Rock Hudson was *not* gay. That's *ridiculous.* Now you're just trying to upset me.

I myself know exactly what I'm going to look like and act like as an old lady. It's probably from all the Geritol I've taken over the years, but I've got my Chico's wardrobe all picked out, and I totally know that I'm going to do a lot of gardening and pretending that I'm cool with the fact that my children never call me, and that my daughter-in-law is a harpy who marginalizes me in the life of my son. My hair won't be gray (I've already decided), because then my husband elder-Jason won't have elder-sex with me. But it *will* be appropriately peppered with lowlights and cut in a shapely but easy-to-maintain bob.

When I think about these things, which is now basically every day of my life, I am reminded of my grandmother's influence. Every time I do poochies by my desk at work, or congratulate my two totally platonic (I'm positive!) male friends (who also happen to be roommates!) on their amazing ikebana creations—and marvel that no woman has yet been able to capture their hearts—I give a nod to my Gam. Sometimes, when I hold my breath for ten seconds after someone in my vicinity sneezes, to prevent inhalation of their mucus, just like she taught me, I think of her and thank her for teaching me about the importance of evading tuberculosis molecules on public transit. And whenever I look down at my rapidly aging hands, I am reminded of how far ahead of other people I am when it comes to accepting my fate. Because of her good work, I'm already like a little old lady in a little *middle-aged* lady's body, and I'm almost okay with it. I may wear push-up bras and dye my hair, but my panties are . . . comprehensive, and my feet just come *alive* in Birkenstocks. I'm halfway there.

smooth criminal

A person can get away with anything if they're dressed well and act like they belong, even when they don't. This is an important thing to know if you live in a place like New York City, where the shabby are judged sharply and stalked by in-store security like they are at a checkpoint on the North Korean border. The lesson of *Pretty Woman*, in which the hooker with the heart of gold actually *can* afford to buy all the clothes she wants and, therefore, deserves good service in those snooty stores on Rodeo Drive, just like anyone else, has not been taken to heart here. At the first whiff of a home-spun manicure, no one will look at you, no one will serve you, and if you happened to spontaneously combust, no one would walk across the aisle to pee on you to put out the fire. You won't merely feel invisible; you will be actively scorned. And it's not your imagination. You might as well have just pushed a shopping cart of old soda cans into the store and eaten a live cockroach that you plucked out of your own cleavage. The mail-order bride behind the counter probably killed her own grandmother to get here and she's not going to waste her time giving a free makeover to the unkempt lady in the sweatpants.

You always hear stories about people walking out of department stores having shoplifted canoes and freezer chests and things, and when you ask how they got away with it, the answer is undoubtedly "no one thought to stop them." It's partly a confidence game and partly a testament to the person's physical appearance. And although those stories probably never actually happened, they could have if the thieves were well-groomed, nicely dressed, and looked like they could afford a canoe if they wanted one—or at least exuded an intimidating air of confidence that discouraged anyone from asking to see a receipt at the door.

I've been analyzed unfavorably by retail workers since I first entered adulthood, stopped wearing makeup, and got my first, but not my last, Anne Murray shag haircut. Now shopping makes me feel emotionally fragile, the way some people feel when they shop for bathing suits. For me, shopping is like a purgatory in which I am *eternally* shopping for a bathing suit; only in this case, everything is a precious, hand-crocheted, white string bikini two sizes too small. Only super-bitchy drag queens will serve me, while blatantly twittering about the cellulite above my knees.

The air of haughty self-confidence I try in vain to project is as flimsy as the fabric in the bias-cut dress that a shop owner once refused to let me try on, because my body type wouldn't have "looked right" in it. It was difficult to take a principled stance on that one, with my lower lip quivering uncontrollably and my eyes filling up with hot, wet shame. When I bought my last pair of running shoes, which I typically buy on the basis of expensiveness (important) and a cool color combination (essential), I was asked, "Are you *fast?*"

I couldn't tell if the sales clerk was talking to me. "Are you talking to me?"

"These shoes are for fast people. If you're not fast, they're not right for you." As in, *I'm looking at you and I can tell that you don't run fast. Fast people don't shop for running shoes with a Java Chip Frappuccino and a baker's dozen of Timbits spilling out of their fanny pack. I can tell you just want those shoes because they're orange.*

"Yeah . . . but . . . they're *orange.*"

These kinds of confrontations flummox me. Why would this woman *care* who was buying the shoes? Wasn't she working on commission? Was anyone really expecting *Mercury* to amble into The Running Room in a Sunday post-brunch haze to peruse the latest in jet-fueled shoe-wings? And why was her obvious yet irrelevant disdain for me penetrating my soul?

Of course, I immediately had to tell her my entire life story because I am compelled to by blood. Like my mother, and her mother before her, at the first crack in our "confident shopper" facade, we are required to give too much personal information to people who don't care about us and think we are basically hillbillies—thereby confirming for them that we are, in fact, hillbillies.

"Well, fast, I don't know. I mean, I have been running for many years. I recently had a baby, so I'm not running that much anymore. Haha! *Muffin top!* Did I say that? Anyway, who's got the time for running with two kids? Uh, not me! But I guess . . . hmmm, fast, well, not fast exactly, not *not* fast, though. I mean, define *fast*. I did a ten-K with my dad a few years back and, let me see, what did I do that in? Let me think . . . well, my time wasn't bad. You know what, let me call my dad. He knows more about it than me. [Now I'm dialing my phone.] He just ran the Chicago Marathon, which is so great considering he tore his Achilles tendon a few years back. By the way, I eat opossum. Would you care to share my lunch of neck bones and gravy? It's an old family recipe. I live on a swamp . . . my only toy growing up was a corncob."

Of course, as I age I understand that my already tenuous hold on all of these skill sets will progressively erode to the point that I just give up and start wrapping myself in old drapery. Until they invent turtleneck Spanx that extend from just under my chin to the tips of my toes, all public excursions will be met with dread and spontaneous eruptions of perspiration from glands I never knew existed. I get it. I no longer fit in anywhere, nor can I ever get away with anything ever again. But, let me assure you, it wasn't always this way.

For a brief time, as a teenager, I had an acute understanding of how much you can get away with if you look like you're "going places." My first boyfriend and I spent our days dressing like Hickey Freeman catalog models and financing a lavish lifestyle from the profits of a brief teen crime spree. Although, instead of stealing canoes, we stole cars, and instead of doing teen things like dropping acid and fucking, we ordered bespoke shirts and threw parties in expensive hotels for other teens.

I mean, don't get me wrong, we were *doing* it. Everyone was doing it. We were fifteen years old, for God's sake—by the standards of our circle of friends, waiting so long to do it practically made us Amish. I accelerated from Barbies to full-score sex in less than three weeks with an enthusiastic can-do attitude, only to find, sadly, that there were no real surprises in store for me on the flip side of my virginity. Except for the realization that once you "broke the seal," no subsequent high school boyfriend would accept the answer "No" again without a superhuman amount of whingeing on his part.

Sex with my first boyfriend was a little bit like learning how to put in a tampon, but only half as enjoyable! I could have taken it or left it, to be honest. I took it, I found it boring, and after we broke up, it took years and many successive relationships before I even remotely felt like trying it again. Together we generated the kind of sexual chemistry that occurs when a sea cucumber sits motionless on the cold, dark ocean floor and dreams about dry-humping a nearby scallop.

But we had much bigger plans for ourselves than just being mediocre lovers. Why not try our hand at being mediocre criminals? Me and my Dapper Dan boyfriend fancied ourselves a modern version of Bonnie and Clyde. If only Serge Gainsbourg had known about us! He surely would have written a song about us, too! We were pretty sure we were "just like them"—kind of cool and counterculture, crime committing, and "a couple," although we had no knowledge of their story, the things they did, what era they lived in, or the violent and controversial way in which they were killed.

We felt like rare birds in a sea of dirty street pigeons. We knew that we were leagues ahead of all the other teenagers because we had a "life plan," which basically amounted to living in a car until we could start our own crime syndicate in Miami Beach. But we looked so good together in our coordinated mint green oxford shirts and madras shorts that no one could deny we were moving up in the world. I carried "an important bag" of fine horse-bridle leather that he bought for me, and wore the kind of sunglasses even my parents couldn't afford. We once went an entire year without wearing the exact same outfit twice. It was very romantic.

Obviously, we were idiots.

We would sit for six hours on the phone, sometimes overnight, not saying a word to each other, just breathing into the phone. My mother would quietly agonize over our extreme stupidity in the next room, and pray that no emergency would befall us that would require her to wrestle the phone from my hands so that she could dial 911. When we weren't busy listening to each other stare into space, all we did was argue about whether or not I was a slut. I said no, he said yes.

Because he was Eastern European, he knew for a fact that all Canadian girls were sluts. This was a known fact in the Eastern European community.

I would cry unstoppably: "But you're the only person I've ever had sex with!"

"I know! Only a *slut* would have sex with me!"

"Well, what does that say about *you*? Maybe *you're* a slut for having sex with *me*!"

"I'm *supposed* to be a slut. I'm a boy. *You're* just a slut."

"How do you *know* I'm a slut?"

"Because you have slut *tits*."

"What are *slut tits*?"

"The tits of a *slut*, stupid."

When he was mad at me he would call me "slut tits," which drove me to hysterical fits of rage that often ended with me threatening to hurl myself down some sort of embankment.

He was decidedly unattractive, with a big nose and tiny, dark, closely set eyes that gave him the appearance of a skinny dog you might run into on a beach vacation. At first you would feel sorry for it and throw it a piece of food, then you would be slightly annoyed by its perseverance, and in the end, even the most peaceful dog lover among us might be inclined to beat it to death with a stick. His miserable personality, I figured, was the result of a life lived without sufficient parental affection. I vowed to give him the love he needed, no matter what. It probably would have been better for all of us if one of my tight, loving hugs had ended up gently smothering him to death.

He wasn't brown skinned, but he was definitely ethnic enough for my grandmother to find him confusing and scary. For one thing, his name was barely pronounceable, even for the most cosmopolitan among us. The dearth of vowels made it impossible for my grandmother to speak his name without twisting her mouth into an awkward grimace. This was a woman who had trouble with the word *Perrier* when ordering it in restaurants, so any attempt to say my boy-friend's name just made it sound positively menacing, like the name of some rare disorder.

He and his family wore their heritage proudly. So proudly, in fact, that it was his ethnicity that drove the deep-est wedge between us, taking our shabby teen romance and elevating it to the level of Romeo and Juliet, let's say. Star-crossed lovers who were meant to be together but were torn asunder by the prejudices of their families.

He was Croatian, and his parents *hated* me. I mean, they *hated* me . . . partly for distracting their son from his nonexistent studies, but mostly for not being Croatian. They loved everything about Canada, except for the part about it not being Croatia, and thought all Canadians were idiots and chumps. Their big thing was making fun of the type of food they imagined Canadians eating for Sunday dinner, all processed and studded with marshmallows. I tried explaining that our national diet was a *lot* more varied and interesting than that, and that yes, ambrosia *did* qualify as a dinner salad because it was supposed to be served on *lettuce leaves*. Anyway, what did Croatians like to eat that was so nutritious and authentic? It's one thing to feel disliked, but these people practically drove me out of their house with torches and pitchforks when I came over for lunch one day and admitted that I had never heard of Provolone cheese. His family was really into their cheese.

My boyfriend and I had a huge argument about it afterward.

"It's not even Croatian!"

"It doesn't matter. Everyone knows what Provolone cheese is."

"But I've never had it before . . . !"

"I know. My parents think you're stupid."

"But my parents don't keep it in the house! How would I have even known about it?"

"Well, then your parents are stupid, too. Stupid *cakes*."

Even though he was Croatian, he liked to call Canadians "*mangia* cakes," like all the second-generation Italian kids did. It made reference to the belief that we pasty Anglo-Saxon Canadians were just a bunch of pathetically lapsed Catholics who didn't believe deeply enough in transubstantiation. Therefore, to us, eating the holy host was as sacred as just "eating cake," which is to say, *not* sacred at all. In a roundabout way, it meant that we as a group were lacking in culture and proper values; that we were a gormless blob of laziness and low standards. I once asked him what he thought the expression meant, and all he said was, "It's because you like to eat *cake*, stupid slut tits."

Anyway, all over his house were pictures of the Pope and President Tito that followed you with their eyes, and after his parents caught me messing around and trying to make their precious portraits come to life, that was it. I was forbidden to enter his house ever again. It wasn't a difficult exile for me. As far as I could tell, all they ever did was despise other cultures and yell at one another; though in retrospect, I think that was just their style of talking.

He was banned from my house, too. I think my mother was afraid we were going to "make unregulated whoopee" all over the place and that I would end up pregnant, just like she had in her teen years. Her strategy was to take away my house key, so that even *I* couldn't come home. I don't think she really thought it through, because in the end, all it did was drive our activity underground, beyond the reaches of any parental interference. We had no choice but to find creative places to satisfy our most suburban desires—to fornicate unsatisfyingly and to hold dinner parties.

Enter crime.

He started out as kind of a lowbrow thief. Fencing car stereos and whatever he could get his hands on. I found this endlessly cool, because it meant that he always had money in his pocket and never had to get a job working for "the man" like I had to do. I don't know how it happened exactly, but his thievery escalated to the point that he started stealing cars for a living and using them as his own for long periods of time. Later he would sell off whatever he could from them.

I was his lookout girl, the *accomplice*, the one with her eyes bugging out of her head and making bird sounds in the designated parking lot, while trying not to slip and fall in the sweat dripping off her upper lip and pooling at her feet. I wasn't very good at it, but still, we never got caught. A fluke, for sure, but I took it to mean that I was a criminal master-mind, and the whole time we were together I knew I had an *incredible secret* that made me *special* and *cool*. I never gave a single thought to the immorality of the whole endeavor—to the idea that stealing was wrong in any way, that my actions would one day come back to haunt me, that people worked hard for the things they possessed, and having some snot-nosed kid rifle through them in a deserted Dairy Queen parking lot was extremely unsavory. I literally thought it was a victimless crime, since in my worldview, owning a car in the first place automatically made you a fat cat. If you were rich enough to own one car, surely you could get another. I mean, these things were insured, right? Big deal! You'd probably end up with a brand-new car for your trouble! Lucky duck . . .

I don't know what the hell I was thinking. I mean, *we* had a family car, but we weren't exactly fat cats. If someone had stolen our car, it would have been a *huge* issue. A major crisis. Although, as far as I could tell, there was no great black-market demand for boxy cars from Communist coun-tries, so I think we were safe. Our family car was the antith-esis of design and desirability. It was like driving Hitler's mustache.

We may not have been rolling in dough, but we also weren't poor. It's not like I couldn't afford decent clothing or had to steal food to stay alive. There was absolutely no justification for my participation in these crimes. I suppose it was a combination of teen narcissism and minor-league thrill-seeking that inspired us.

But I can't deny that I did love snooping through other people's glove compartments and personal effects, and integrating them into my life. Wearing their shoes, eating their crackers, and making fun of the mix tapes they had spent hours dedicating to their loved ones. I still have and use a good-quality stainless steel stockpot that I took from the back of someone's car. The person whose car we stole must have been so confused, because they eventually got their car back intact, but with no stockpot.

"Who would steal a *stockpot?*" they must have said to themselves. "What possible use could a thief have for a *stockpot?*"

Well, let me tell you. Even thieves like to make turkey soup from time to time.

Anyway, my boyfriend was responsible for all the real dirty work, for all the *actual* criminal activity, but I benefited the most. Neither of us even had our driver's license yet, but he would hot-wire the cars so that we could drive them around as much as we wanted without a key. We drove carefully, so as not to raise any red flags with the police, and took great road trips anywhere we wanted to go. Then, guided by inner voices that would tell us when the car was getting too dangerous to continue using, we would abandon it on a busy street and walk away. Of course, not before selling off any valuable parts, which he would do, and then I would rent a hotel room under an assumed name, and we would throw a big party. At the time, you could pay cash for any hotel room without leaving a credit card, and he was too shy to do it himself, so that was my job.

We went to expensive hotels only. I would put on my best, most preppy outfit and forge into the lobby like my parents owned the place. I always wore a diamond ring on my ring finger because—and don't ask me why—I figured I could pull off the look and that it would be more convincing if everyone thought I was married. I didn't want to be regarded as a hooker.

As if anyone at the front desk ever believed I was a "Mrs. Rosewell," which was the name I always used because I thought it sounded sophisticated and rich. My hair was cut shorter on one side than the other, I usually wore white Bermuda shorts with two or three polo shirts layered on top of one another, and I had *braces* on my teeth. I was fifteen but could have easily passed for eleven. When I see photos of myself from that era, I think I look like a miniature sociopath—the kind who is able to play a relaxing round of tennis after stabbing her classmate to death with a pair of toenail clippers. Nobody would have ever mistaken me for either a wife *or* a hooker, but they always rented us suites anyway, and gave us long, bemused looks as we walked by, arm in arm, talking loudly about the state of disrepair at our "summer home."

In any case, I'm sure they weren't thrilled by the steady stream of teenagers who would later mosey through the lobby with bags of chips and six-packs, on their way to our room. I would organize cocktails and snacks in one area, and he would be the greeter, leading people through the place like it was our condo and we were the Onassises, if Aristotle Onassis had come from a long line of dry-walling contractors whose brains were addled by too much exposure to toxic caulking compounds.

Everyone knew and appreciated how precious and unique it was to have a hotel room to party in, and we demanded that people respect an appropriate noise level so that we wouldn't get kicked out and lose all of our money. We did get ejected from a hotel once, for getting it on in the fire stairwell. Our sex was obviously so no-frills that they probably didn't even identify it as such, but they kicked us out anyway for looking like we were "up to something" in an off-limits area. Perhaps they were too embarrassed to give it a name, it looked so rote.

My parents never figured out the exact nature of any of my delinquent activities, but they knew *something* was going on. They were convinced that I was on drugs, though nothing could have been further from the truth. My boyfriend and I had a pretty strict "just say no" policy in place, and though we would have been happy to sell you the subwoofer from the back of a Volkswagen Golf we had just jacked from a hospital parking lot, we would judge you pretty harshly if you tried to "spark one up" in our presence. Drugs were for losers. And Canadians.

In fact, much to the confusion of my parents, I was like a roving one-teen antidrug crusader around my own home. Whereas other kids were busy rifling through their parents' stashes and gleefully diminishing their supply, I was deliberately and dramatically flushing it down the toilet and reprimanding my parents for their youthful disregard for drug laws. And drugs were expensive then, too. My parents did a *really* good job of hiding it all; they *sensed* that I was after it, but for all the wrong reasons. Nothing could compare to the youthful vigor I applied to rummaging around in their private stuff to find incriminating evidence against them. With the methodical thoroughness of a CSI and the maniacal determination of an SS, I ransacked whole rooms for evidence of their drug use—like a junkie looking for smack, except that if I had actually *found* smack, I probably would have called the police on them and initiated the process of emancipating myself, just to be a bitch about it.

By contrast, if they even dared to move my jacket from the banister into the closet, I considered it a personal violation punishable by a twenty-four-hour tirade of teen angst, concluding with a hunger strike and something nice and passive-aggressive like leaving the freezer door open overnight so that everything in it would melt.

It never occurred to me to actually *try* the minuscule amounts of pot that I sometimes found or to even sell it, which I easily could have done. My rebellion came in the form of long-winded lectures delivered just when my parents needed their dope the most to calm their jangled nerves;

for instance, when being confronted by their fifteen-year-old daughter saying things like, "Guys. It's your *attitude* that determines your *altitude*."

Assuming that I was on drugs was just wishful thinking on their part.

There's no question that my boyfriend brought out the worst in me, but I had never looked better. And thank goodness, because it really diverted attention from my main hobby, which was skipping school for great swaths of time. I became a master forger of sick notes, and combined with my innocent appearance, no one was the wiser as we spent almost every day joyriding and breaking into his house while his parents were out to watch space shuttle catastrophes or *The Price Is Right*.

Only after I blew off exams before Christmas break in tenth grade did I feel threatened with exposure. This was surely something that would have repercussions and necessitate a call home from the school authorities. Maybe even a parent-teacher meet-and-greet. I could hardly afford that.

My plan was to break my writing hand and pretend it had happened days earlier, thus having rendered me physically incapable of completing my exams, retroactively. No one in my family had seen me for about a week; by that point I was more of an apparition around the house, coming and going after dark, occasionally plundering the supply of cheese while everybody slept, so I figured I had a good chance at pulling it off. Time was of the essence, of course, since I had already missed all of my exams without having provided the school with any excuse for my absence. My boyfriend accommodated me by bashing my hand over and over with a rock as it rested on the fender of a stolen car. I was so relieved when a big swollen egg popped up and I was able to go to the emergency room! Naturally, we did it at one o'clock in the morning, because we had procrastinated all day. But when we finally did the deed and walked into the ER with big smiles on our faces and a broken hand, we must have looked like the Grady Twins.

Of course, none of the hospital staff bought our story. I claimed to have fallen on the ice, but the type of injury made things very obvious. It must have been perplexing for them when I learned that my hand wasn't actually broken and I registered disappointment. It seemed to me at the time that a simple sprain was going to be a tougher sell to my parents and the principal of my school. Surely the hospital staff thought that my boyfriend was physically abusing me, and yet, for all that, no one called my parents. Two kids in the ER in the middle of the night and no one called home.

To be fair, I *was* wearing my pearls.

When I got home at four o'clock in the morning on a school night, I shoved my mother awake and coolly hissed: "I missed all my exams. I sprained my hand. Expect a call from the school. Go back to sleep."

Later, I withdrew from the high school I had been attending and transferred myself to a different one, close to my boyfriend's trade school. No one seemed to care that my parents hadn't made the request; they released my school records to me, and the new school accepted me without so much as a peep to my legal guardians. I delivered that news to my mother in the middle of the night as well.

Though my parents tried, no matter what they did, they couldn't keep me away from my boyfriend. His verbal abuse and questionable morals were powerfully alluring to my teenage brain. Eventually, though, I'd had enough.

My father had insisted that I attend the wedding of a close friend out of town, and I adamantly refused to go. My boyfriend had demanded that we spend the day together, knowing full well that I had an important family event to attend; he loved to stir things up in my home life and found any conflict involving my father especially delicious. As usual, he threatened to break up with me if I didn't do as he said, which was just about the worst thing I could have imagined at the time. Conveniently for him, I failed to notice that he never seemed to follow through on all his idle bullying.

I railed against going to the wedding and made up a million excuses, but my father was wise to me by then. Naturally, he was hoping that my boyfriend would break up with me and detach his Croatian proboscis from our family for good. Confronted with anger on both sides, I decided it made the most sense to simply kill myself, so that everyone in my life would suffer as greatly as I had in this cruel dilemma that had befallen me. That is to say, having to go to a wedding when I really didn't want to.

It would be great! They would all be so sad! I, of course, would be dead. Nonetheless, as my final breath approached, I would have the opportunity to savor the sweet smell of victory, which would make everything totally-totes worth it. No note would be necessary. Everyone would know what they had done to me.

I drank a quarter cup of Pine-Sol, took six Correctol laxatives, and waited for death. For good measure, at the last minute, I popped in a videotape of *The Killing Fields* and lay down on the couch, so people would know that in my heart I was very smart and socially aware. As I slipped away, into what I hoped would be a deep, deathly slumber, I recall questioning the logic of killing myself with stool softeners on the newly upholstered sofa.

Eight hours later, and I had miraculously lived. My father and stepmom were home, buzzing about, getting ready to go to the wedding, oblivious to my personal suffering. In the end, they made me go, though I had terrible diarrhea and my breath smelled like pine resin. I was too ashamed to tell them what I had done, and since no one was likely to be checking the supply of ladies' laxatives in the medicine cabinet for missing tablets anytime soon, thankfully my bungled suicide attempt went undetected.

A day or two after the wedding, my boyfriend threatened to break up with me again, and this time I just let him. He had just worn me out. I gave him his stupid bag back, stopped dressing like Phyllis Schlafly on the set of *The Love Boat,* and started obeying the laws set forth in our society with respect to stealing. If anything, I threw myself headlong in the opposite direction, finally embracing the life a normal degenerate teen would live. I traded my roughly hewn Slim Jim for a roughly hewn apple bong, started smoking hash like the poppy fields were going out of business, and let the spring "resort wear" catalogs pile up in my room, at long last, unread.

penis envy

I have a knack for penises. Or so I've been told. What I mean is, if a penis could talk, I'm pretty sure that's what it would say to me, anyway.

I shouldn't brag, even though it's totally true. I suppose a lot of people could make that claim to one extent or another, because let's face it, penises are a pretty forgiving lot; they're not at all picky as long as you show an interest in them first. They're so eager for attention from someone other than their owners that they'll do anything to make that possible. A penis is a fair-weather friend at best, but for some reason it's always sunny in Bee-town. And I don't mean that as a compliment.

I'm not in any way referring to my level of sexual expertise here. I mean, I suppose if one ended up in my hand or something I'd know what to do with it, but I'm not exactly what you would call a Penis Wizard. In my experience, it's easy to get penises on your side if you're planning to do something sexual with them, but that's not the point. I'm talking about something much more subtle. I just have a *way* with penises. They want to be in my life.

Penises follow me wherever I go; to be more specific, they reveal themselves to me. When I'm around, they can barely be contained by the zipper of a simple pair of cotton chinos. How they love to taunt me.

And I'm not suggesting that I have invited this kind of attention on a conscious level, because I haven't. But if you have a penis, and you're excited by the prospect of taking it out of your pants and fiddling around with it in front of a stranger, the odds that I am the stranger in question are very high.

If you've ever dreamed about serenading an innocent person in the park while strumming your guitar, with your foot up on a tree stump as you free-ball in your shorty-short jean shorts, I am definitely the girl you would want to do that in front of. Just in case your penis needs a breather, let's say, and it prefers an audience. I'll be over here sitting on my beach towel, quietly trying to enjoy my vampire-based romance novel, in case you're interested. Which you are.

Recently, I undertook a casual census among my friends with respect to random penis exposure. It happens to us all at one time or another, but the sheer quantity of strangers' penises that I have seen in my lifetime put everyone else to shame. And believe me, I shamed them.

I should point out that none of these spontaneous viewings have occurred under threatening circumstances, so I can't claim to feel traumatized. I don't hang around in scary parts of town, I don't lurk in dark alleyways waiting for perverts, and I don't have a sign on my chest that says SHOW ME YOUR JUNK. I don't walk around with my boobs hanging out of my shirt, or pantless in chaps, tacitly asking men to reciprocate. And I hardly have a "come hither" look to my face. As one of my ex-boyfriends once helpfully pointed out, I look "kind of ugly from far away but basically cute when you get up close," and I have "the gait of an ape," so I don't imagine these men are scoping me out from a distance as a prize to be either conquered or urinated on in some weird *National Geographic Special* version of courtship.

Most of the time I'm simply sporting mom jeans and a scowl, trying my best to get from one place to another without encountering any brazen genitalia along the way.

I don't get the feeling that any kind of sexual encounter is being asked of me when these penises dart out at me from every direction. My participation in the exchange is limited to innocent bystander or, perhaps more accurately, victim of a drive-by. Nobody asks me to grab them, or go anywhere with them, or fuss with them in any way. It's quite simply, "Hey! Look what I've got!"

There isn't even an interesting leering expression on the faces of the men doing the flashing. Often they appear quite gentlemanly and avuncular, neatly dressed like golf pros in pink Tommy Bahama pants with the little embroidered palm trees on them, or businessmen in suits, hurrying off to their important luncheons, briefcases in one hand, penises in the other. They could be someone's grandpa for that matter, with frosty old-man hair peeking out from beneath their knit old-man hats. And withered old-man penises peeking out of corduroy old-man pants. Usually it's just a nod of the head and a smile. "Top o' the mornin'" or "Am I going in the right direction, miss? I'm trying to get to Broadway." And there it is, bobbling around between us, ashamed, trying its best to sneak back into its master's slacks. It's hard for me to maintain my sense of outrage when I notice that the flasher is wearing Wallabees and old-timey sock garters.

I often wonder how it is possible that this has happened to me so often, it has become boring and routine. Where's the thrill? I long for the days when I would look at a stranger's penis and think, *Now* that's *something you don't see every day,* or, *Ewww!* and not just, *You might want to get that mole checked out.* It has come to the point that I now make eye contact with the fully clothed and feel disappointed when they don't put on a show.

Something deep inside of me simply encourages people to pull their genitals out of their pants and put them on view. That's my personality quirk, and whatever the reason, there it is. And it's not always as simple as a geriatric exhibitionist flashing me his Good & Plenty on the street. Unfamiliar penises find their way to me in a variety of ways.

In high school, I had a job at a customer-service call center for a video vending-machine company, the kind you find in a convenience store where you could put in your credit card and walk away with a movie. Business was good, even though at the time it cost like $150 for a beaten-up copy of *Ladyhawke*. People put all kinds of crazy shit back into the machines instead of the movies they were returning. We got lots of movies that belonged to other video stores, and things like tampons and cat turds and, one time, a bundle of twigs meticulously cut to the exact length of a chocolate bar and sealed perfectly in an empty Mars bar wrapper.

One of the main things people would pop back into the machine was homemade pornography. It was one of my jobs to sort through all the videos and log the first five minutes so that, in case someone called to claim their video, we knew which one they were talking about. I guess the end goal was to get *our* movie back, and the company felt that the best way to do this would be through superior customer service. There weren't *that* many machines in existence, and since I was decidedly the least squeamish of all the customer-service reps, most of the logging work fell to me. Fine. I had seen my share of professional-quality pornography by that time, and had already become inured to its charms. But home-crafted pornography is a completely different animal. It makes a person ashamed to be human.

My video logs went something like these:

Disgusting bleached-blond woman with torpedo-shaped breasts turns camera on. Fat man in purple thong rests on purple bed in background. Woman flaunts genitals in front of camera and reveals "killer bunny" tattoo located above pubic bone. It depicts a cartoon rabbit in Ray-Bans holding an Uzi. The rabbit is smoking a cigarette.

Old man with dirty feet tries to seem like Marlon Brando in The Godfather. *Two women in togas enter the frame and do a striptease to the song from 9½* Weeks. *They also have dirty feet. Man is wearing Ray-Bans.*

Usually people wouldn't call looking for their videos. They were presumably too busy sitting at home with their heads in their hands and wondering where it all went wrong. But there was one guy who did it *all the time* and always wanted his videos back, knowing that someone had seen them. And the person who had seen them was always me.

They were all basically the same:

Shirtless man standing in bathroom mirror takes penis out of jeans and starts grappling with it.

Shirtless man in bathroom mirror takes penis out of bathing suit and grapples with it. Shows us how long it is.

Shirtless man in bathroom mirror takes penis out of sweatpants and plays with himself. Knocks it around a little bit on the bathroom vanity. Shows us how long it is.

A week or two after we took one of his tapes out of the machine, he would call to get it back. He'd ask for a description of the video, at which point the customer-service rep, usually me, would drily read my log back to him.

"Um . . . shirtless man. In bathroom mirror. Removes towel. Dries penis with towel. Shows it from multiple angles . . ."

"What color is the towel?" As if it was anyone but him.

Then I'd ask him to return our copy of *Crocodile Dundee*, or whatever movie he had outstanding, and the exchange was under way.

I wondered what his house was like. I mean, I knew what his bathroom was like from the videos, but what about the rest of it? Did he have art on his walls? Did he like to listen to NPR while he vacuumed? What did his mom think of him draping his dong all over her hand-knit afghans? He had a normal voice. Maybe he was married with kids. I hoped they never went to pop in that copy of *Crocodile Dundee* and had to see their dad wrestling with his genitals to a Bananarama song like I did.

He knew I was required to watch him, and he liked it that way. I guess when you think about it, necessity really *is* the mother of invention, even for people whose "necessities" are, let's say, whimsically perverted. In this case he just needed to know that someone out there was looking at his wiener, so in many ways he was being quite innovative. This was long before we had things like PenisBot to safely guide us through the journey of amateur porn. So . . . kudos to him.

Later, while working as a receptionist for the federal government, I had a coworker who dated some rather salty characters. She was pretty salty herself. Often she would run out to the parking lot for her cigarette break and brag that her boyfriend had just fingered her in the backseat of her ratty old minivan. I didn't doubt her. She always came back from her cigarette breaks looking quite flushed and refreshed, and she really never smelled like smoke at all. Come to think of it, she always had to gobble down a sandwich at her desk after lunch, too, so she was probably getting poked over *that* break as well.

Although I wasn't exactly jealous of her, her ability to get her rocks off at any time of day in any place she found herself certainly made me feel like I was missing out on something. Why didn't taking down messages from angry taxpayers all day make me as wet as it seemed to make her? Next to her I felt like a big, unsexy blob. A crone. A lady turnip.

So when she asked me to go out with her one night to see a show her boyfriend was in, I was (a) extremely surprised and (b) (strangely) flattered. Clearly, she could see that deep inside my nerdy exoskeleton was a hot, *libidinous* nerd who was ready to party. I was eager to have some of her kooky mojo rub off on me. No matter that her boyfriend at the time was a stripper in a ladies-only club named LyppStyx.

Prior to that my only connection to the club had been to burst out laughing every time I passed by. Strip club names without proper vowels bring me such joy. But now I took it seriously. Was it to be a sexy, Lypp-smacking [*sic*] journey down the river Styx for me tonight, or just a big ole basketful of . . . um . . . man-Styx that we would all want to put our . . . Lypps . . . on? Ewww. The spelling bee winner in me was going to have to let down that tight hair bun *tonight* for *sure*! Abandoning my struggle to decipher any coherent meaning behind the name of the place, I went in and prepared myself to be impressed by what I imagined to be hordes of glistening tan-skinned Adonises. With their "extremely desirable" penises hanging out.

By this point in my life, I was definitely over the shock of being startled by a random penis, so by facing them head-on I figured I was being proactive. *Bring it on,* I thought. I still had some weird idea that I was going to impress my coworker with my uninhibited Friday-after-work self.

Turns out you can still get flashed in a strip joint.

The place was a filthy, neon-lit hellhole that looked hideous and smelled sour, like a potent goulash of dirty dishcloth, Love's Baby Soft, and taint. Its customer base appeared to consist mainly of menopausal receptionists who would get shit-faced on Amstel Light and wait in line to make out with the strippers. Why they would have wanted to was another matter entirely.

The strippers themselves were as charismatic as a pile of soiled paper plates. They all had thick French-Canadian accents, greasy mullets, and lifts in their boots. If they could have counted thirty teeth in all of their mouths put together, I would have been surprised. The "hot bartender" who was the ringer, the one who was supposed to keep you drinking all night, sported a do-rag, a bolo tie, and a raging case of bacne.

Now, I don't know if you've ever spent time in a ladies' strip joint. There's no question—they're as terrible as gentlemen's clubs, but in a totally different way. In gentlemen's clubs there's usually some dreary music playing and some poor stripper alone onstage, grinding away to it, while the other ladies, usually high on something, push drinks and lap dances on the lonely and/or horny and/or befuddled clientele. If the men try to touch the women, all hell breaks loose. The bouncers get involved and there's pushing and shoving and screaming, and it's all very chaotic and aggressive.

At places like LyppStyx, strip joints that feature men dancing for a female client base, the men still run the show, but in a much more subversive way. The women are encouraged to touch them. They are permitted to make out with the strippers, who further tease the women by getting very physical with them—to the extent that a man with a ladies' haircut and sparkle dust on his shoulders can really get anyone excited—and the women *really* seem to get into it. It's very interactive. All I could think at the time was: *Ladies, you might be barking up the wrong tree here* . . . but it wasn't until I saw their performances that I knew for sure I was right.

These guys thought they were real entertainers. You could tell they had a lot of stretching sessions and conversations about what awesome professional dancers they were. In lieu of regular, boring old stripteases, they did themed ensemble pieces. Some contained social messages, others were strictly fun, but all of them involved group choreography and extreme gayness.

There were a lot of jazz hands and fedoras involved. They did a *Grease*-style "high school cool crowd" scene to a Bill Haley and the Comets song that featured nude men partnering with each other at a sock hop. Like, with lifts and drags and everything. And as the marquee event of the evening, they did an environmental commentary in which they all played homeless people and street sweepers who, after holding hands and coming together to clean up the Earth, eventually just ended up ripping their clothes off to the song "Another Brick in the Wall." There was no question in my mind that they were all boning one another.

The women went crazy for it. When I went to the bathroom, I was overpowered by the scent of female hormones that all those middle-aged women before me had shed; garbage cans were overflowing with paper towels used to blot all the hot-flash sweat.

There was a lot of penis going on, but none of it was very enticing. I couldn't leave, because I didn't want to seem like a pussy, but as I sat there in my seat, I could feel the "uninhibited me" leach out, only to be replaced by more inhibitions than ever before. *Could* a person get crabs from a bar stool in a strip joint even though she is fully dressed? What's to stop the crabs from nestling into the seams of her pants and hanging on until she gets home, when they could get to her exposed pubic area? It was mortifying.

My "friend," sensing my growing dismay, invited her boyfriend to come over to the table to loosen me up a bit. He trotted over in short white cowboy boots and a mauve cock sock. He was about four feet tall, with LyppStyx's trademark teased and frosted hockey hair, and a tiny mustache to suit his tiny skull, which probably contained a tiny brain the size of a greyhound's. This was not the sexual dynamo I had pictured, satisfying her at mandatory union break after union break. He looked like he would have needed a step stool to get up to her vagina.

Now, I haven't had sex with a *ton* of men, but I do have a couple of rules governing my choice of partner. One is that you may not ever call it *making love*, or I will throw up. But the other, *more important* rule is that you may not have sex with me if your hips are narrower than mine. If you put on my jeans, and you are swimming in them, then you are not the man for me. It is not going to happen.

This guy could have set up shop in my jeans, raised his tiny family in the pockets, and traveled around the world in a lettuce leaf using the leftover fabric of my jeans as the sail. At any rate, he put down his little stool (I *knew* he had a stool!), climbed up on it, and started gyrating beside me with his penis about two inches from my face. I didn't ask him to put his penis in my face, and yet, unexpectedly, there it was. He slowly pulled off his thong so that I could marvel at his great gift. And my friend was loving it, really getting into it, squirming in her seat: "He's got a great cock, *non?* It's really wonderful."

I struggled for a response. "I like how it has . . . girth."

I was having trouble picturing them together. If she got on top of him, I had to imagine that he would snap like a twig, so I focused on his little cowboy boots, which had obviously been hand-me-downs from an older sister. I wondered if he had teeny-weeny cloven hooves inside those boots. He did sort of remind me of a jaunty little French-Canadian Pan. I appreciated his efforts to "drive me wild," but at that point I was considering a move to lesbianism.

Anyway, I was buying cigarettes for my friend at the vending machine in the lobby, when the guy who comes in off the street to sell roses *flashed me*. In a *strip club*.

I was exhausted. I had just spent twenty minutes trying to have a conversation with my friend's boyfriend, who, despite all my protestations, had knocked his balls into the side of my head for three entire "dances."

I just didn't have the energy to scream at the flasher or yell for security. And besides, the "security team" was just a bunch of tanned strippers in peekaboo bikini briefs and heels. So I took matters into my own hands.

"Thank God you're here. Get on top of me right now and force-feed me all of that man meat!" I shouted at him. "Your penis is irresistible to me! I must have it inside of my body right this minute!"

I started to back him into a corner. "No, don't put it back inside your pants! I require all of the services you are offering me. I request that you inspect my vaginables and see if they meet your exacting standards!"

As I pulled my own pants down, he ran out of the building, never so scared in his life.

I mean, a penis is one thing, but who would ever want to take a look at someone's *vaginables*?

may december never come

There's really nothing creepier than going somewhere with one of your parents and having people think you are together, as a couple. Of lovers. Who do it. With each other. The only way to describe how this makes me feel is to say that *it makes my vagina nauseous,* if that's even physically possible.

I mean, okay, I get it, it's hard to blame anyone for coming to that conclusion. The world can sometimes send mixed messages. Someone sees a young person with an older person who's not *that* old, maybe they're holding hands or linking arms or something, and it's natural to think the worst. For those of us who had teen parents and there isn't much of an age difference, it's actually quite feasible. But when you see the look of disgust that creeps across their faces as your dad says good-bye to you, planting his chappy dad-lips on yours . . . Oh, God. You see? Just writing it down made my vagina throw up.

Recently I took my mother to the site of Woodstock, the site that commemorates The Great Embarrassment of my mother's life. With ample opportunity to attend the concert—in fact, she was in New York at the time on a rare visit from Canada—my mother spent Woodstock weekend, the event that defined a generation and changed music history, on a cashmere sweater–set shopping expedition with her grandmother. She completely missed her chance to be cool. By the time my mother decided that she, too, was ready to jump on board the hippie train, everyone else had already packed up their water bongs and gone into finance. She could try to hide it all she wanted, but I knew that growing up she preferred the music of the Monkees to the Beatles, and I found it hilarious.

I took hundreds of photos of her looking wistfully across the green field, photos directly intended to fool people into thinking that she had been there and was reliving one of the most special, most uninhibited times of her life. When you look at the photos, you can practically feel her conceiving me in a sweet, patchouli-scented lovemaking session with a mud-spackled stranger. I kept reminding her that at the precise moment "history's biggest happening," as *TIME* magazine called it, was taking place, she was in a Bonwit Teller dressing room about ninety miles away, locked in a battle of wills with her grandmother over whether to get the coral or the turquoise set.

As we argued over her participation in my freshly conceived photo-essay entitled *Cardigan Calamity,* a car pulled up and a smiling, gray-haired couple got out and the woman wandered over to us.

"Isn't. This. Something?" said the lady, looking out over the vista. You could tell that she had been there at the actual concert and was remembering something really delicious and life altering.

"It surely is." My mom sighed dramatically to indicate that she had been there and that it had been transformative for her as well. I was practically bursting with the desire to rat her out and started to smirk uncontrollably.

The lady kept going with it. "What a beautiful tribute. This is just great. How nice to have a place to come back to, where you can stand and take a picture . . . and remember . . ."

"What was *your* favorite part about that weekend?" I asked my mother. "Was it avoiding Central Park so that you wouldn't get stabbed with heroin-filled needles as you walked around, or just the part where you shared a double bed with your nana?"

My mother chuckled knowingly. "Hey, man, weren't we all just a bunch of squirrels back then . . . trying to get a nut?" Her eyes misted over as she looked at the monument. I was hoping that it was with shame over that awful metaphor.

She continued. "It was quite a time . . . quite a time. So insanely far . . . out."

I felt my mother gird her loins against further mockery as she tried to come up with more vague comments to fool the couple into thinking she had been there, too. I had to respect this character trance she was in; she was really giving it her all. It was amazing how well she could simultaneously fake a collective memory *and* use only the bulging tendons in her neck to threaten my life.

Then the man sauntered by. "Do you want me to take a picture of you and your *partner* together in front of the monument?"

Record scratch. Spit take. Comical sputtering. Woman relentlessly making fun of her mother is instantly silenced by elderly do-gooder.

Listen, I don't care about being thought of as a lesbian. I mean, it's not necessarily the first conclusion I want men to arrive at, since I like to consider myself in possession of *some* vestigial remnants of heterosexual attractiveness from my pre–child-rearing years, but I could live with it. At this point in my life, I should really embrace *any* acknowledgment of myself as a sexual being. I just don't want to be accused of being caught up in a May-December romance with either of my parents.

My mom was the one who was smirking now. I could tell she took it as a compliment that they thought she was unique and lesbionic, but it meant only one thing to me: an old man had just spent at least three seconds imagining my mom and me doing the scissors together, and when he revealed that to us, *I* then spent at least three of the longest seconds of *my* life imagining my mom and me doing the scissors together. If you've ever had an aquarium, you know that fish can die from a disease known as "ick," and that's precisely how I was starting to feel.

So in the spirit of human dignity, can we all get together and agree on just this one thing? That henceforth, old and young people are not permitted to bump genitals. There must be no more cross-generational pollination. Okay? That way, no one will ever again accuse me of being my mother's lover, and no one will get queasy when I kiss my dad in public. I never want to hear a waiter in a restaurant ask a man, "And for your lovely daughter . . . ?" only to find that they are on their honeymoon. And I never *ever again* want to hear that someone Larry King's age is capable of maintaining an erection and/or putting it anywhere near anyone who was born after 1990. Time to hang a little sign on that thing that says CLOSED FOR BUSINESS.

Am I alone here? Everybody basically knows that it's yucky when the young date the old, right? Even though most people have thought about it at one time or another, there's still something nasty and primeval about it. You sort of imagine the old person desperately pawing away at the younger person's flesh, trying to figure out a way to switch skins and start over. Listen, I'm not above imagining myself rubbing warm coconut oil on an intern or two, but that's only because I am trying to keep them supple for when I finally figure out how to switch skins with them. The hyperbaric chamber I sleep in to keep my face looking taut is only going to go so far—it's not my fault we made the conversion to HD. My motives are wholly aesthetic, and therefore pure.

But for the rest of you, you are shamelessly trying to steal that other person's nubile young life force, and everyone knows it. It's confusing. It causes social awkwardness. It's flat-out gross, and shame on you for even thinking about it.

Furthermore, there are those of us who are married and don't get out much, and you are ruining our date nights. We have young children, and we do not like to be subjected to thoughts of sexual situations that involve the kind of much-too-old person who is out there waiting for our kids to meet minimum legal age requirements for consensual sex. We do not want to go out for Thai food and a movie and have to spend our whole night eavesdropping on your conversation to try and figure out if you are parent and child or a creepy couple, and whether your casual touching is a loving parental caress or just a prelude to an evening heavy with ass play. And a person who is out with his or her parents should never have to be subjected to the kind of scrutiny and judgment that we will inevitably send their way. We're from Canada. We're known for our *searing* looks.

If you're already old and considering branching out into the youth population, please stop and rethink things. Find someone your own age to besmirch. Believe me, you have nothing in common with the young. They may pretend to think it's okay, but they really don't much care for the music of Jimmy Buffett, they don't consider him "the musical Mark Twain," and anyway, they're not even really sure who Mark Twain was. And they are totally going to judge your body and notice all the "old" things that are going on with it. Like how you have gray hairs in your pubic thatch, and how your knees are kind of wrinkly.

Maybe you have some skin tags, or you've had some pre-cancerous moles removed and you have scars that look a little like cigarette burns but could just be bedsores or un-explained old-person lesions. You probably have some kind of digestive stuff going on by now, too, and that means you do things like actually give some thought to your regularity and have back pain if you walk too much. I bet your fridge is even full of probiotic yogurt. You can try to pass it off as regular yogurt, but we all know what it's really for, and be-lieve me, a young person will, too.

I mean, they're going to pretend that they don't see these things or that they're not important, but that's just code for "I sure hope you're as rich as I think you might be." And when they find out that you're not, because you probably aren't, they're going to start telling their friends how boring the hospital was that time you had to pass a stone and worry-ing about the day they're going to have to start cutting your toenails for you when you can't bend down anymore. You may not even really be *old* yet, but you're still old*er*.

It's not really fair, but there it is.

We all know someone from high school (usually a girl), who dated some old guy (always a teacher), who was proba-bly married with children, and they had a long, tumultuous affair and everyone thought it was gross except them. They'd sit there in typing class and he'd call on her from time to time in this sort of ironic tone of voice, using her first name and *middle* name, or address her with a big sarcastic *Miss* in front of her last name. "*Miss* O'Brien, congratulations on being our first-place typing triathlete for the second week running." "*Catherine Mara O'Brien* . . . I'm going to have to keep you after class if you keep this up!" Chuckle, chuckle. And everyone knew that the two of them were definitely going to be humping all over your independent-study projects later that evening. And that *she'd* probably end up grading them, wearing one of his big shirts, as he photographed her smooth young ass. But in the end she'd just meet someone with less baggage and more potential than a career typing teacher, and move on.

Full disclosure: I tried to date older for a while.

I was feeling vulnerable. I had just been broken up with over the phone by someone I barely cared about. His exact words were, "I ain't jokin', woman, I got to ramble . . ." And I was like, "Are you kidding? You *know* I know that song, right? Are you actually breaking up with me by reading me the lyrics to 'Babe I'm Gonna Leave You' over the phone?" I was so mad I could barely keep it together. It's one thing to date someone you don't even really like, but when they like you even *less* than you like them, that's just not fair.

"*Ramble?* Do you even know what the word *means?* You've never called me *woman* before!" And then he started sobbing and wailed that he was "the devil in disguise" and that he "couldn't be trusted." That's when I really laid into him. I could tell that he had been cheating on me and was trying to break up with me using my own patented technique of pretending to care *too much* about the other person to *allow them to continue dating me.* I should have beaten him to death with my high-heeled shoe like an Atlantic City tranny would have.

At any rate, I was ripe for the plucking when Jim came along. He seemed very together, very accomplished, or so I thought. In retrospect, I think that it was only the contrast between my lack of accomplishments and his full-time job that made his one-bedroom adults-only rental condo seem like Dionysus's yurt at the peak of Mount Olympus. The first time I went over there, I was like, *This is it. I could live the rest of my life here. He's got laundry machines. And his own car, with parking.*

I wasn't completely sure, but it occurred to me that "adults only" probably meant it was going to be a Hedonism-style cavalcade of pleasures, maybe even with a Japanese fuck swing in the common area. I mean, how could you have children on the premises if every Sunday afternoon "penny social" was really just an orgy waiting to happen? I wasn't necessarily planning any erotic escapades with Jim, but it was nice to know that there were options.

As it turns out, the whole place was a purgatory for gray-haired widows and divorced men, content to eat frozen dinners and watch *Deep Space Nine* until they fell asleep alone and covered in potato chip crumbs. Sadness wafted everywhere you turned. Through the long, quiet, hideously carpeted hallways. Past the lonely men in slippers taking their tiny bags of garbage to the incinerator with the little handwritten sign urging you not to leave it sitting in the chute. I found out that in actual fact "adults only" just meant that there was a nurse on the premises who could restart your heart and administer your diabetes medications if you forgot to take them. What I thought was a sex swing was actually just a pulley system that old people would use to help maintain flexibility in their upper backs. They would sit in a chair and operate the pulley overhead, while the nurse would watch for the person's spine to lose its integrity.

I should have known things weren't going to work out for me and Jim, mainly because I wasn't that attracted to him in the first place. But I was a struggling actor and I thought that if I could just fall in love with someone who had a real career, then maybe I could give up waiting tables for good and focus on my many undiscovered talents. Most of which I thought were lying dormant inside of me due to my shabby living situation, but later came to realize simply didn't exist. What I didn't understand while I was busy concocting my plan to retire at the age of twenty, was that *I* was a part of *his* plan to stay young forever and never ever die.

Whenever I spent time with Jim, I felt hunger emanating from him. Not necessarily sexual hunger but the kind of hunger that made me think he might want to make a Samantha suit, put it on, and dance around nude in front of a full-length mirror. I started to notice that he never laughed at anything unless I laughed first and that I got to pick all of our outings. I suppose he didn't want to be accused of choosing something for us to do that would have seemed old, like attending a Rich Little show or doing word jumbles.

I tried *so hard* to fall in love with him, but it was just impossible. I couldn't overlook his innate uncoolness, how hard he always tried to seem trendy and weirdly tough and more knowledgeable than me. I discovered that when older men try to dress like Kurt Cobain, for example, they really just end up looking sad and homeless. He would always say things like, "If it wasn't for this hip, I'd probably *still* be playing professional football," despite the fact that he had *never* played professionally and was about five and a half feet tall and downright portly. The surest sign that you are too old to date a young person is when you start incessantly talking about your hips. Young people don't usually have to think about their hips. They just work. And they don't understand why yours don't.

I'm sure that in his day, his breath was sweet and his hair lush, but in truth, age changes a person internally and externally. Fifty-odd years of living does a lot of damage to a gut, and no matter what you do, it starts to seep out at the worst possible moments. Once you've got old-man stink on you, it's tough to get off.

Incidentally, fifty-year-old men shouldn't run around thinking they can "take" twenty-year-old men, either. They shouldn't have to! Fifty-year-olds are at the point in their lives when they should be taking comfort in the material wealth they have accumulated, driving their canary yellow Corvettes willy-nilly with the top down and the wind whipping across their bald spots—not getting nervous diarrhea from the fear that their twenty-year-old girlfriend is going to ask them to get into a bare-knuckles brawl with some young ex-boyfriend hooligan. Because if it does happen, I don't want to have to be worrying about those creaky old hips of yours.

At any rate, Jim was always saying this crazy stuff to me about his lunatic aspirations in the field of extreme sports. How he'd love to pick up BASE jumping now that he had the time, how one day soon he was going to head down to the Nutcracker for an "epic crank," and how much he fantasized about living in "Cabo-Wabo" just like Sammy Hagar. He imagined himself "dropping out" of society and living in a "palm tree bivvie" on some beach somewhere and rolling spliffs all day.

At first, I fell for it. God, I wanted to believe I could get into it, I really did. I knew I could be a kept woman, I just *knew* it. Living in some crappy-assed bivouac in the middle of nowhere wasn't exactly on my to-do list, but I could definitely picture myself puttering around a beautiful garden somewhere, snipping fresh herbs for our salads, working only on artful passion projects that were perfect for me as an actress and spoke to my newly christened philanthropic interests. I'd have to convince him that we needed a home base with unlimited hot water and cozy featherbeds from whence to plan all of our daring exploits.

A potential relationship with Jim spoke to my softer side. The side of me that wasn't afraid to let others make tough decisions for me and write all the checks and give me a huge allowance that I would spend only on impractical purses and lingerie. There was a lazy little lady inside me eating Cheetos to pass the time, and it was time for her to emerge and take over for a while.

The first time I visited his apartment, I was underwhelmed but stayed positive. I attributed his modest surroundings to an earnest desire to keep the space Zen-like and minimal. I thought maybe he *liked* living in a place that resembled the most basic room at a Holiday Inn Express because it kept him humble, kept him on his toes. He didn't have time to worry about things like "decor" and "comfort"; he was too busy sitting on a mountain of money and staying nimble. A person who lived like that could be called away at any time to go live in France or Bali and they could *just leave*, with no strings attached.

When I arrived at the door, he greeted me, gave me a little kiss on the cheek, and said "I'll be right back," as he slipped into the restroom. Very debonair! I thought he was going into the powder room for a quick pee and a little freshening up. But after standing in the kitchen for what felt like an inordinately long time, I started to worry. Then I heard him, quietly at first, but growing in urgency and volume as time passed.

"Oh, dear. Oh, my goodness. Oh, heavens."

"Hah. Oh . . . ouch, ow *ow* . . . oh, hell . . ."

"Dammit! Oh, for God's—*sake*. Ah. Ahhgh."

I had no idea what was going on and I started to panic a little bit. I knocked softly on the bathroom door, and then began to pound on it when he didn't respond immediately.

"Are you okay in there? Do you need help? Do you need me to call someone?" I thought he was having a seizure, or a heart attack. "Do you need me to call 911?"

The whole time I was thinking, *Please don't die . . . please don't be dying . . . I can't be a person who was semi-dating someone when they died on a toilet . . .*

I pictured him clutching his heart and doubling over in pain. I hoped that if he was having a heart attack, it would be minor and the reason he wasn't responding to me was that he had merely knocked himself unconscious on the bathtub. Pretty soon I was going to have to be a hero and burst through the bathroom door to save his life. It would take him weeks to recuperate. In that time, I would have to take a break from waiting tables to drive his awesome car all over the place, running errands and picking out new drapes for the condo. If absolutely necessary, I could put my grandmother's dresser with all my stuff in it right in that corner . . .

And then, sweet as pie, from behind the door, I heard, "Nope! I'm fine! Out in a sec!" Surely he must have been sitting there the whole time, hunched over the bowl, listening to me panicking in the other room, and praying to die of embarrassment. On the contrary, when he emerged from the restroom, nothing in his demeanor suggested that anything out of the ordinary had just occurred. Instead, he just enveloped me in a big bear hug, and we went out to dinner. Where he *ordered* for me.

"She'll have the coconut shrimp." And then he helpfully explained to me, "It's shrimp, but with coconut all over it, and then you dip it into a spicy sauce. Have you ever had *shrimp* before?"

Old Samantha would have pounced on that like a fat kid on a Smartie. I mean, really now, a lesson in delicious undersea creatures and savory flavor combinations? But this was the New Me. I decided to allow him to feel like he was teaching me something. After all, wasn't this part of the charm of dating someone older? I went for it.

"Sounds neat! I hope it's not too spicy!" I was really laying it on thick, and he loved it. I liked this new me! I was going to catch me a husband and live in an adult community and start wearing long, flowing tunics and making canapés.

We went to one of the *Star Trek* movies, and it was terrible, but I could tell he loved it and wished he were half as smooth as Captain Jean-Luc Picard. I made fun of it afterward, and he gamely tried to join in, but I could tell he found it sort of hurtful that the idea of a bald, middle-aged sex symbol just didn't seem credible to me.

As our relationship progressed, it was becoming less and less likely that my plan was going to come to fruition. For one thing, I started to grow weary of receiving life lessons and could no longer condone pretending not to know the answers to things. I was beginning to think that, even though I was half his age, I had actually done more with myself and had a higher IQ with respect to life intelligence. I took to calling him sensei any time he tried to tell me something I already knew and had actually learned by fifth grade. I don't need my boyfriend informing me that the most nutritious part of the potato is actually the skin. Or that Michael Bolton wasn't the original singer of "(Sittin' on) the Dock of the Bay."

It didn't help that my best girlfriend started calling him Speckles behind his back because she happened to see him in a swimsuit and thought he looked like a toad. Plus, the generation gap was starting to reveal itself as more of an impassable gorge. Jim's favorite story to tell, for instance, was the lamest thing I had ever heard, but to him, it was pure poetry.

He had traveled quite a bit in his time, and on one memorable trip to Spain, he met a Spanish woman who captured his heart. I guess they had a steamy affair or something, because just as he was set to return to Canada, they had this windswept midnight walk on a beach that was incredibly romantic, according to him. At one point, she just whipped off all her clothes, grabbed his hand, and started running in the sand and shouting, "Jim! Have you ever known how to be alive?"

Whenever he told that story (which was frequently), he seemed so dreamy and emotional, as if he spent every day on a quest to live life to the fullest in honor of her grand question. To me, it seemed like there might have been some kind of language barrier going on. For one thing, the question barely made sense. I needed clarification as to what she was alluding to, and how nude running could ever increase anyone's enjoyment of life. I have never tried it, as I am sure no good could ever come of it. Just imagining myself doing it makes my boobs hurt. And let's face it, shouting the word

"Jim!" has no romantic qualities whatsoever, *especially* if you are in Spain, because there it comes out sounding more like "Jeem!"

In short, his story was too gay for me. And by "gay," I mean old-timey gay. Like how all the characters in *The Music Man* are lighthearted and gay and full of merriment, and how I would never want Shipoopi to pull off her clothes and run with me down a dark beach littered with jellyfish.

The last time we went out, I ran into a friend from college who called him Mr. Bee. It was embarrassing for both of us, but we tried to slough it off and enjoy the night by pretending not to notice that everyone thought I was the world's most undateable girl, out on a Saturday night holding hands with her dad. But I finally realized that I had to break up with him when he covered me in poo dust for the final time. Being accused of dating my dad was one thing, but I was getting tired of delaying my dinner plans because he needed to answer the call of his unstoppable bowels.

I have a thing about walking into bathrooms after people have defecated. I know that no one really likes it, but I *really* don't like it, because it makes me visualize myself getting covered in a thin film of poo residue from the person before me. I always feel like if I can sense its presence, if it has worked its way up my nose, then it is a tangible thing and is somehow now all over my jacket.

So he really sealed the deal when he gave a repeat performance of the crazy bathroom behavior I had seen for the first time only weeks before. Hello, how are you? Back in a flash.

And into the bathroom he went. I don't profess to know what was going on in his lower intestine, but suffice it to say that he put up a valiant struggle. It sounded like he was being ingested feetfirst by an anaconda.

"Oh God-*damn*-it *hell*."

"*Why?* Jesus, oh, *oh, ow no! No!*"

"*Help*. Aagh. *Why are you doing this to me? Please*. STOP."

First of all, I questioned the efficacy of talking to the poo and begging it to stop. It was just plain futile. I also questioned the relationship know-how of someone who would make a twenty-minute pit stop on his girlfriend's toilet, battle loudly with the poo for supremacy, and saunter out as though nothing had happened, and then expect to walk right out the door and paint the town red. You can't just yell at poo and pretend it never happened when the other person is ten feet away in a studio apartment.

And the dust! My God, the poo dust! Every time he left the bathroom after one of his "episodes," he seemed to want to walk swiftly into a tight embrace with me. He would drag that dust right out of its birthplace and anoint me with it.

I couldn't take it anymore. I had no interest in being so up close and personal with his bodily functions, and I knew that if the relationship were to continue, then *my* relationship with his movements would only grow more intimate. I was done. I wanted to date someone who could eat curly fries and not have to make love to a bottle of Pepto-Bismol right afterward. I was weary of breath that smelled like chewable Rolaids and the sight of orthotics by the front door. I wasn't prepared to think about things like ulcers, and I didn't care that the doctor had found benign polyps inside his body, or that his drink of choice was always vodka and cranberry juice to promote drunkenness with just a little nod to prostate health.

So while Jim was laying cable and, in the process, completely contaminating all of the towels in my bathroom with his dust, I had to think fast to avoid another fecal embrace. Since we both ran (or in his case, walked) with different crowds, I wasn't worried about running into him at a party or a nightclub, so it would be relatively easy to let him down gently with a plausible little white lie. Or the words of a song I once knew. As he emerged from the nuclear dead zone that was once my bathroom with the fan running (at least he was considerate) and came toward me with his arms spread wide, I turned away from him and felt a kind of peace envelop me. I summoned all of the phony tears I could muster.

"Stay away from me, Jim . . . I'm like the devil. Um, in disguise."

He looked confused. I had never rebuffed one of his pooey hugs before, and so I continued. "You see, the thing is . . . I got to go away from this place. In fairness to you, I've got to quit you."

"Are you breaking up with me?"

"I don't wanna leave you . . . Jim. But the truth is, *man*, I've got to *ramble*."

I explained that I'd been given the opportunity of a lifetime and would be leaving for Switzerland in a matter of days to study with Mummenschanz and just couldn't in good conscience make him wait for me since he was in the winter of his life and should be devoting the time he had left to perfecting his freestyle BMXing and/or acing large-print crossword puzzles. He took the news like a man, and then, after waddling to the front door like Charlie Chaplin, turned to look at me one last time. I smiled and mimed pulling my face into a frown before waving good-bye. Who needed a man to take care of me when I had *these* kinds of acting chops in my arsenal?

sailor moon

People do all sorts of things to benefit humankind. Some of us are healers who work tirelessly to overcome insurmountable challenges and bring relief to the needy, the sick, and the disenfranchised. There are those of us who work to keep the peace, those who keep us safe from harm—servants to the public good, who lay their lives on the line each day so that we may go about our mundane existences blissfully ignorant of the dangers all around us. Others among us dedicate themselves to making the world a more beautiful place: From nothing, they create great works of art or music that bear witness to the human experience, and in doing so move and inspire us from one generation to the next. I, however, am not one of those people.

The official designation I give myself is Lady of Leisure. I love to putter. I can fritter away long swaths of time doing things like reading recipes, filing recipes, imagining how good a certain recipe might taste, and then hunkering over the sink to consume a partially warmed tray of chicken nuggets. I'm excellent at spotting brunch nooks and putting my feet up. If I could, I would spend all of my remaining days taste-testing chocolates, while a team of six-year-old girls gently brushed my hair. Left to my own devices, I'd probably end up like one of those Chinese emperors who let their fingernails grow six feet long and curly, while attendants sponge bathe their undercarriage.

Unfortunately, due to a terrible accident at birth (i.e., not being born to people of means), I am forced to fight against my most basic nature and work for a living. Hard to imagine, I know. Trust me, it wasn't easy growing up and watching from the sidelines as other, less worthy people obliviously buzzed about, living the life that I was meant to live.

For years, I was forced to endure the spectacle of the other teens at my super-WASPy high school, their skin tanned *in the winter* from skiing at Zermatt or Gstaad. They would complain about the lack of good television in Switzerland and how the food was gross, so "rich" and "fatty." I would just chuckle knowingly, as though I had been there many times myself, and say things like, "*Tell* me about it. *What is with* Switzerland? Switzerland *sucks ass!*" And in summer—their skin tanned from tennis and poolside lounging, mine beleaguered and pimply from the fried-chicken spatter at the snack shack where I worked—we'd sit around in their backyards writing explicit love letters to their gardeners as they quietly groomed the topiaries.

Every once in a while I would pore over my baby pictures, looking for some clue that would lead me back to the family I was so obviously stolen from at birth. The family of architects who designed their house around a beautiful tree that they didn't want to remove. The family of engineers who played Scrabble competitively and composed original songs for one another for Christmas because they didn't want or need anything else. The family with the summer compound that was luxurious and impressive, until you realized that you'd only seen the boathouse. That was where I belonged.

But every year I returned to school from summer vacation practically translucent, like one of those phosphorescent cave-dwelling fish that live so deep in the ocean, humans can't even get to them. It was embarrassing, but this was my lot in life—I was a worker drone, biding my time until the universe recognized my gifts and led me to that exalted place where others would fry my chicken for me.

The less work I tried to do, the worse the jobs seemed to get, and things didn't improve much once I got to college. Applying for a job at a framing store in the mall, I was asked to describe my perfect job. The question threw me for a loop because I had never imagined that a job could ever be described as "perfect." Did anyone have a *perfect* job? Were there people out there who actually *enjoyed* working for a living? Was the manager of a Frameworxx franchise somehow implying that the job they were offering was *perfect*? And was she *really* expecting me to feel that way, too?

Golly Gumdrops, I don't know where to begin! My perfect *job? I guess what would excite me would be the idea of getting up really early and driving to a suburban mall half an hour before it opens, for some light dusting and heavy contemplation of the train wreck that my life has become. I would hope that it would involve some kind of hard physical labor, like hanging ornately framed photocopies of cherubs on the wall. I'd also probably enjoy being on my feet for eight hours straight, selling discount frames to ugly people, with an adult-contemporary soft-rock sound track cycling in the background at all times, for not a* penny *more than minimum wage.*

I considered it humiliating to even have to apply for a job in the first place and had pre-decided to look down on the person who was interviewing me, just for insisting on an interview. I mean, couldn't they have just given it to me for showing up? I had to have been the only applicant, right? Fresh out of management school and drunk on the smell of Cinnabon, the store supervisor insisted that I oblige her. I could tell that the next question on her list was going to be "Have you always been interested in working with frames?"— for which I had no answer that she wanted to hear.

It took me five minutes of awkward silence to come up with an answer, but upon careful consideration, I told her that my perfect job would entail spending the day in a cushiony room, napping with baby animals. Maybe they had been abandoned by their mothers or left by the side of the road; whatever their situation, it would be my job to keep them company and pet them and generally give them a warm,

I KNOW I AM, BUT WHAT ARE YOU?

motherly vibe. When they wanted to play and roll around on the floor, I would do that with them, and then when they got tired, they could fall asleep in the crook of my arm or snuggled in my blouse. And sometimes I would give them a warm bottle, just like in all the nature specials. But they would definitely have to be baby animals. I wasn't about to get scratched or nipped or anything—I'm no St. Francis. Also, weirdly, the job would pay a lot more than you might expect.

I took the Frameworxx job to pass the time as I awaited that life-changing phone call from the Animal Rescue and Snorgling League. I couldn't believe that the framing store actually hired me. I must have been the only interviewee without hooves.

Although there were no baby animals on the premises, there were plenty of soulful photos of seal pups for sale, as well as a generous assortment of photographs of wolves peering out from behind trees. It was a regular who's who of framed Successories posters—the seal obviously a symbol of dedication to a common purpose and general cuteness, the wolf signifying the untamed spirit and encouraging mysterious originality.

Formerly a person of good taste, I found myself falling in love with anything framed, as long as it weighed in at about three hundred pounds and looked vaguely baroque. I recall enthusiastically using my employee discount to buy a massive gold-framed print of two postcoital leopards. I originally intended to hang it over my futon bed, but I thought it sent the wrong message to all my potential suitors. It ended up hanging over the computer, and for three years there it stayed, always on the verge of falling off and crushing me as I typed. Every so often I would catch people's puzzled expressions as they looked at it, and I just knew that they knew I was an asshole.

The store was managed by one of those women with a slim upper body and pretty face, but with an ass so wide that it seemed like a miracle of physiology. It was confusing. Perfectly normal from the waist up, and then she would sidle out from behind the counter, and boom! I spent most of my time picking up frames that Daniella's ass had brushed onto the ground as she passed by, oblivious to the carnage behind her. She spent all day applying sparkle decals to her nails and affixing inspirational Post-it notes to the staff corkboard: "YES!!" "Drink Other People's Milk Shakes!" "Live One Day as if You Were a Baby!" (I had to assume that meant living on a liquid diet and sitting around in your own shit all day, which I already knew I was capable of doing.)

My first impulse was to feel sorry for her. It wasn't her fault, and really, if you thought about it, wasn't it sort of like a disability? I optimistically decided that she was "differently abled" in the area of ass size, which meant that she was *gifted* in the field of sitting comfortably. But it wasn't too long after she said to me in earnest, "If you've got time to *lean*, then you've got time to *clean*," that all of us started calling her Bummiella.

We used to touch up all the gold frames with one finger dabbed in cheap crafting paint, and one time, Bummiella returned from the ladies' room with golden sparkly nostril rims. The fastidious gay man I worked with went limp with "the vapors." When he recovered his senses, his disgust was electrifying. Every time she reached into the communal snack bag from that point forward, she unknowingly claimed the bag permanently for herself.

Our star artist was a tortured Spaniard named Matteo, who airbrushed canvases in shades of mauve and pink and was pretty liberal with his BeDazzler pen. He was prolific, a living picture factory whose pieces had all the creative energy of something that he had painted while being fellated. I refused to call him an artist, but *he* certainly referred to himself as one, and tried his best to go down in a blaze of glory like one of the greats. Matteo smelled like sauerkraut and was such a raging drunk that one day he urinated on our coats in the staff closet, thinking he was in the bathroom— Bummiella's faux fur got the worst of it.

The people who liked his art were sassy retirees in matching husband-and-wife sweat suits who got most of their exercise by mall walking. They'd stand around the store with their carpet samples and fabric swatches, rapt by his sparkly purple dog droppings, saying things to their mall-walking friends like "This is the Matteo we're considering." I was lucky to get fired when I did, because my dismissal coincided exactly with the day I started to not hate his work. Had I worked there one moment longer, I probably would have become his muse.

I couldn't blame Bummiella for letting me go. She was sick of watching me escape to the urine-soaked coat closet whenever customers came into the store, and I had grown tired of being the only person in the store physically capable of going up a ladder. I had taken to hanging every picture in the store ever-so-slightly askew at exactly the same angle. Bummiella would ask me about it and I would pretend that I had no idea what she was talking about. Maybe I was growing an aneurysm in one side of my brain? It was time to part company.

To be fair, I come from a short line of rather selfish, lazy sluggards. Well, really, it's just me and my father. He works for a living but resents every minute of it and, even though he's well into his sixties, is convinced there's got to be an easier way. My dad searches for shortcuts to wealth and latches onto them about ten to fifteen years after the bubble has already burst. The other day he said to me, "I've been thinking. Why not put some of your comedy skits on the Internets [sic], and I'll manage the website and sell advertising on it? I can quit my job and do it from home [translation: in my underpants], and see where it takes us! Really get your name out there!"

He loved to build web pages with irrelevant icons that he had pilfered from other annoying websites: dancing frogs, tie-dyed peace signs, a dog wearing an astronaut's helmet with a wagging tail and a thought bubble that read *Woof*.

"You know Jason and I already work in television, right?"

"Yeah, but this way, people might actually *watch* you!"

Getting something for nothing is kind of a pet project for my father. If he were at Costco, busy shoving free food samples down his pie hole, they could literally remove the roof and turn it into a Thunderdome and he wouldn't even look up. He'd still be devising a way to make a fifth pass at the lady with the mini chicken taquitos without alerting her to the fact that he wasn't actually going to be buying any today, or any other day.

About five years ago, my father solemnly brought me downstairs to his computer workstation and began explaining a complex network of passwords and international telephone numbers to me; the implication being that should he die suddenly, I would need to know where the money was in order to begin the process of collecting on his extremely lucrative investments. Upon further investigation, I learned that my father had invested all of his money in the Latvian stock market, which was "bursting with opportunity," and he would probably be able to retire at any moment, sitting on a mountain of freshly printed Latvian currency.

And retrieving his money would be easy! All I would have to do would be to decipher the Voynich manuscript, get myself to a pay phone with $100 in quarters, and start leaving messages for Kristaps at his apartment in Daugavpils. Eventually he might return my call at the pay phone, at which point he would internationally wire money to my U.S. bank account in $2,000 increments of Lats. Then I just had to cross the U.S. border, find myself a Money Mart, and camp out there for a week, because, of course, to take all the money out on the same day would seem suspicious. It's illegal to cross the Canadian border with more than $10,000 in cash, so I would need to either take the chance and smuggle it across, or put it in a safe locker and do several cross-border trips over a six-month period of time. Easy peasy, lemon squeezy . . . Until one day, shockingly, Kristaps stopped returning my father's calls entirely. Hopefully, all that money went toward a new MRI machine at the children's hospital in Riga, but I have a feeling it miraculously turned into a new sable coat for a twelve-year-old prostitute.

Later, my father informed me that the man suspected of absconding with all of his hard-invested money was found dead under mysterious circumstances somewhere in the Caribbean. When he found out, he let me know with a mixture of gravity and titillation that our family was now officially connected with "La Cosa Nostra," and that we needed to "watch our backs." It was the happiest day of his life.

The Bees are people with especially superficial aspirations. Every summer, I was forced to take sailing lessons, though we were nowhere *near* sufficiently affluent to own a boat. By my father's way of thinking, it was best to be prepared for the accoutrements of wealth, to brace ourselves for the big windfall with skills such as race car driving and classical dressage, than to actually focus on making the money in the first place. And I tended to agree. Despite lacking all the skills that would provide us with the lifestyle we strongly felt we deserved, we knew that one day we would wear *our own* Top-Siders, actually worn down *by us* from use on our eighty-foot pleasure craft.

I fully expected money to rain down upon me as a reward for the years I had spent cultivating expensive taste in things. And despite my best efforts to remain as soft and tender as the meat of a milk-fed veal calf, my hands were beginning to show the hard work I was routinely being subjected to. An ugly pattern had emerged in my life, and it showed no sign of reversal; an inverse relationship between the amount of work I wanted to do and the quality of the work itself had become apparent. What had happened to my plan to nuzzle kittens for a living? If this was going to be the pattern for the rest of adulthood, I wanted no part of it.

But when I got a job as a penis-clinic intake technician, I thought I was on to something. Yes, I know, "penis intake," I get it. It seemed easy, and it paid better than anything I had ever done before. Plus, I knew my way around a penis by that point, and being a "technician" at a "clinic" seemed like a natural complement to my love of amateur medical diagnoses. My job was to field calls from men experiencing erectile dysfunction. We were encouraged to speak softly, to listen with a nurse's objectivity, and to use the letters *ED* when referencing their penis problems. We were supposed to then advise them of our procedures at the clinic and schedule an appointment, the length of which was directly related to how "dysfunctional" they were. Meaning, did they just need a prescription for Viagra, or did they need to consider the installation of a rod that would create an artificial sort of erection that kind of . . . weirdly . . . worked.

After a lot of blood, sweat, and tears, and long after any sensible person would have given up hope, I had to ask myself, Was all the effort really worth it? The answer, apparently, was a booming, resounding, deafening yes. If there's one thing I took away from that job, it's that a man will literally do anything to save the life of his penis and its various accoutrements—no matter how dilapidated its condition. And let me be clear, this phone line was not intended to be used for phone sex. It was an *actual* clinic, run by *actual* sleazy doctors who knew they could make a lot of money by focusing specifically on a man's inability to give up that particular ghost.

I would estimate that 60 percent of the people who called in were straight-up jerking off. They always let you talk a lot, and sounded vaguely like they were whimpering or straining to put their socks on while standing up. Around 30 percent of them had young mistresses with whom they couldn't keep up, *or* they had mistresses with whom they *could* keep up, they just couldn't get it up for their wives at home. The other 10 percent or so included the elderly and infirm who, against all odds, just couldn't bear to give up the ability to penetrate others with their penises. I was terrible with them. I found it vaguely distressing that I had to field calls from ninety-year-old men who were desperate to get into all those granny panties back at the home.

Old people are allowed to have sex, true, but only until they're, say, seventy-five. After that, it's time to Wrap. It. Up. Congratulations! You've had an active sex life for sixty or so wonderful years! Now let's calmly put our genitals away in a dust bag where no one ever has to look or think about them ever again.

Be honest, if you walked in on the decrepit old rooster mounting the sinewy old stewing hen in the roost, you'd feel all icky inside, too. It's disgusting. Well, that's what it was like having to call elderly gentlemen and take them through the particulars of their penis pumps. It was not something I was mentally prepared for. God forbid they should have a priapism that would land them in the hospital. I wasn't really sure what would happen when the ambulance arrived, but I'm pretty sure the EMTs would just beat it against a door frame or hit it with a brick or something.

Also, dealing with the elderly was detrimental to the calm, Zen-like mood we were trying to create at the clinic. There's nothing like giving life-changing test results over the phone, loud enough to wake Rip Van Winkle.

"Hello, Mr. Jacobsen. It's Samantha from the men's clinic."

"*HEL-LO?*"

"It's SAMANTHA. From the MEN'S CLINIC."

"WHAT IS THIS?"

"SAMANTHA!!!! MEN'S CLINIC."

"WHA-A-AT?"

"CLI-NIC!!!! PENIS CLINIC!!!! YOUR PENIS!!!!"

"APPLE?!"

My voice was hoarse, and my neck muscles were bulging with overuse. In any case, I was soon let go. For one thing, I just couldn't stop saying "penis problems." I dislike euphemisms in general, and "ED" just didn't cut it for me. How do you expect to fix your penis problems if you can't bring yourself to call them "penis problems"? Nobody really seemed to appreciate my tough-love approach.

It was the worst three days of my working life.

Jobs I have considered: professional jewelry thief, professional auto thief and jewelry fence, lawyer, drug dealer, high-priced stripper, high-priced hooker. High-priced anything, really. But it was the job at the bingo parlor that actually led me somewhere promising. I worked there on Fridays, selling tear-off lottery tickets and colorful dabbers to fixed-income pensioners and gambling addicts.

That's where I met Celeste. She was about three feet tall, Vietnamese, and chain-smoked kreteks, holding them between her two middle fingers like a Gestapo officer. She claimed to enjoy bingo and was in attendance like clockwork every Friday afternoon.

Celeste had the air of a sophisticated mamasan in a colonial Vietnamese brothel, barking orders at us like we were her white orchids and a high-ranking GI had just popped in for a quick fivesome. I could never understand why she would frequent our low-rent establishment, until she asked me if I wanted to become a card dealer in her illegal casino. Celeste had been keeping herself busy poaching clients from every game she could find—high-end, low-end, it simply didn't matter. Whether you had a welfare check to blow or your grandkids' inheritance to put on the line, she was your gal. In the entire time I knew her, I never once saw her smile.

The night she asked me to come work for her, there was a particularly tawdry scene at the bingo parlor. An old lady playing bingo with three generations of family members had started vomiting on herself about a third of the way into the game, and her family didn't budge. To be fair, neither did she. She just sat there, dabbing away at her bingo cards while she retched, the vomit spilling out of her mouth, into her blouse, and all over the floor. The family insisted that she wanted to continue playing, and obviously so did they, so I brought the old lady a roll of paper towels to stuff down her top, removed my apron, and walked out the door into the fresh air and a new career as a card shark.

It seemed like a perfect fit. I'd have to work only one, maybe two shifts a week to make all the money I would need, and *bonus!* I would be working in a casino surrounded by high rollers and well-heeled patrons of my future artistic endeavors, should there ever be any. The casino was illegal, so not only would I be making tax-free money hand over fist but I would also somehow become spicy and mysterious. *Double bonus!* When people would ask me how I financed my glamorous lifestyle, I would flash them a sly smile as if to say, "It's best not to ask questions."

It's one thing to feel entitled to a lifestyle that you don't deserve; it's quite another to put yourself in grave danger to accomplish that lifestyle.

From the moment I entered Celeste's "casino"—an unmarked and obviously repurposed office space in an anonymous-looking strip mall—I knew I was taking the kind of chance that even my irresponsible parents couldn't be proud of. Sandwiched between a vacant pita-bread factory and numerous gym-equipment salesrooms that were never open, the casino and its environs felt like the kind of place where a young girl would go to get sold into slavery. And it didn't get any better inside the actual casino.

It was as if a telemarketing office had just shifted gears one day, and all of the employees started dealing blackjack instead of making phone calls. The card games were set up in separate cubicles under the continuous buzz of fluorescent lighting, and the only thing you could buy to eat or drink was sugary iced coffee. There were definitely people there, but they all looked like their spirits had been crushed in utero. Everyone in there was male, middle-aged, and Vietnamese. Nobody really spoke, and if they did, they definitely sounded angry. I know that might seem like a racial stereotype, but in this case, they actually *were* angry, and I know this because it was usually directed squarely into my face, and I deserved it.

My level of incompetence as a blackjack dealer cannot be overstated. I have a peculiar hatred of cards that I was gamely trying to overcome as I pursued my new career. In my civilian life, whenever anyone suggested a card game to me, I would physically recoil as all the card-related synapses in my brain misfired simultaneously. The moment I stopped playing Crazy Eights, let's say, I would instantly forget all of its intricacies, and if we played again, you would have to explain the whole thing all over. It wasn't much better with blackjack. There were too many rules. I could remember the twenty-two part, but I would forget, for instance, what an ace is supposed to represent and when. Whenever people doubled down, or split pairs on me, I just wanted to yell "FIFTY-TWO PICKUP!" and flip the table over.

When Celeste scoped me out, I think she saw great potential in me. My job was to ensure that her all-male clientele kept spending and losing their money at the table, just by being cute and charming enough to keep them playing, and just skillful enough to ensure that the house would usually come out on top. But my inability to remember the fundamentals of blackjack made it difficult to outsmart professional gamblers at lightning speed.

Celeste's disappointment was palpable every time happy customers walked away from my table, their hands brimming with chips. I could feel her eyes boring into me from across the casino every time I tried to sneak a peek at the *Everything You've Ever Wanted to Know About Blackjack* book poorly concealed in my apron. This wasn't working out the way I had planned at all.

I was such a popular destination table, I felt like a pink coconut Hostess Sno Ball in a sea of ravenous, fat Elvises. As soft and delectable as a fluffy pillow, a little too sweet, and kind of stupid, I was sure that all of the men were licking their chops as I set up my little workstation; naturally, I assumed they were trying to calculate the right price for my white ass on the black market. In reality, I was severely overestimating my own attractiveness, and underestimating their ability to identify the intellectually disabled dealer at the casino.

It's not that I was conceited or anything. It's just that I was raised mostly by my grandmother, who believed in me so fiercely that she was convinced I had to beat men off with a stick every time I walked out the door. It wasn't until I was thirty-seven years old that I realized my grandmother had been delusional about the length of my legs. My whole life she had insisted that they were "up to here" and that I was built like a gazelle. She used to stare at me when I was drying off after a bath and just marvel at my leg-to-torso ratio. I'd look at myself in the mirror and agree; I *was* blessed.

But after a lifetime of buying long-fit jeans and then having to get them shortened at the tailor's so that they didn't drag on the ground, I remember the exact moment it dawned on me. I was naked in front of a full-length mirror, and my husband was looking at me as I complained about how hard it was for me to buy pants because of my superlong legs. He burst out laughing. It took me the better part of a week and multiple examinations of my body before I realized that he was right. I had normal legs. Maybe even on the short side of normal. Upon further investigation, I found I didn't have the legs of a gazelle at all . . . rather, at best, I had the drumsticks of a thin turkey.

But for the moment, there I was at the casino, vulnerable, leggy, hopeless. Celeste lost her temper at me one too many times during my on-the-job training. Did she *actually* just shout *"Di di mau!"* in my face? Was there a cellar under the casino dedicated to Russian roulette and were they just waiting for me to really fuck up to justify dragging me down there and betting on the "ultimate gamble"? I was no fool. I had seen *The Deer Hunter*, and I knew that, no matter what, things weren't going to end well.

At the time, I was convinced she was saying, "Shoot her in the head!" but later I found out that *di di mau* actually just means *hurry up*, and she was totally justified in asking me to do that. But that's not the point. She was scary, all her friends were scary, and I just knew that if I stayed there, eventually I was going to end up chained to a pole and slow dancing for spare change with sexual deviants in Ho Chi Minh City. Or getting fired. Probably the latter, but you can never be too careful. So I quit.

That's when I decided to move on to acting. Just like Celeste, my teachers seemed to see me as a person with great potential. And just like my grandmother, they fed me the same line—that with my talent and unstoppable moxie, I'd be a shoo-in as a professional actor. It did seem like a natural extension of my desire to make a career of not working hard but getting paid a lot of money, and since I had no appreciable skill in any other department, I really had no choice but to try.

Cut to me, four years later, a shell of my former self, spirit-gumming a blond anime wig onto my head for a five-day show as a costume character at a rural cider fest. Instead of pursuing an actual career, there I found myself, hard-scrabbling a career from gig to gig as a children's performer at fall fairs and gymnatoriums, waxing on about social injustice to toddlers who mostly busied themselves gripping their crotches and talking at me at full volume about what they did at circle time that morning.

Children's entertainment was a natural fit for me because (a) I dislike other people's children, and (b) I was unemployable in virtually every other aspect of show business. Don't get me wrong, I wasn't about to become one of those people running around in an enormous bear costume or anything. I have it on good authority that those people routinely get pushed into fountains at malls and/or set on fire. I know this because all of my associates actually *did* dress up as Mayor McCheese or whatever, and for them, this job represented a huge step forward in their acting careers. They were just so excited to be able to breathe freely on the job, their heads unencumbered by some seventy-five-pound hamburger cage. I didn't have the heart to tell them that for me this job represented the darkest depths of what I would do for money. Once I had ruled out prostitution and stripping for a living, this was basically all I had left.

The show itself was based on a Japanese cartoon called

Sailor Moon that was a huge hit with girls age two to maybe six. It was about ten girls—obviously, high school students by day and superheroes by night—who would fly around town in sailor suits. That is, if sailors wore suits that were made of shimmery skintight spandex, cut just below the buttocks, and thigh-high fuck-me boots. Maybe I just don't know enough about the Japanese navy, but in *their* country's version of the show, the characters are even younger, and practically nude a lot of the time. Yeah. Creepy.

There was also a sexy witch, the natural enemy of a sailor and ruler of the Negaverse; and a heartthrob guy wearing a tuxedo and a mask, inventively named Tuxedo Mask. The narrative was so vague and ridiculous that it could have been written by a basket of acorns that had fallen onto a laptop by accident. The producers who put the show together were a pair of brothers who put so little thought into it that they basically left the script up to us and then shoehorned in a bunch of dance numbers from a previous gig—a traveling oldies show that they had sold to nursing homes and senior centers around the country. It made no difference to them that none of the television characters ever sang or danced.

The show took about seven minutes, start to finish. We always drew huge crowds, like, in the thousands. But, of course, we usually appeared at the sort of event that involved thousands of people standing around eating food on a stick. Observing our audience gather prior to the show was akin to watching cattle get rounded up into their pens; they would stand there stupidly unaware that if they just used a little teamwork, they could push the fence over and run like hell.

Part of our act was to sing the song "Do You Wanna Dance?" over a vocal track that we clearly didn't have the rights to use. The choice of song was unfortunate because our show was routinely hijacked by teenagers who would bait the younger children to shout back at us. There's nothing really comparable to the feeling of asking two thousand children if they "wanna dance" and having them shout *"No!"* in perfect unison. Fuckers.

In the end, the show was an unrecognizable hodgepodge of David Cassidy music, bad stage combat, and girls in spandex sailor suits trying to hold on to their wigs in the howling winds of the outdoor venues, as we fought over a fake "crystal" that just looked like a child's magic wand.

We would always do a question-and-answer period at the end of the show, and because I was technically the "star" character, I had to field most of the questions. Luckily, anyone over three was *not* permitted to ask me a question, because based on the looks in the parents' eyes, the questions would have been along the lines of "How do you look at yourself in the mirror?" or "How *dare* you put this abortion of a show on a stage and present it to children?" All of the mothers hated it, but the dads liked it. We were so bad, constantly screwing up our choreography, while the buttons on our epaulets popped off our cheaply made outfits. At least all of our stumbling made us extra jiggly in our sailor suits.

One time, we went to a small town and people had to pay

$35 to see us do our thing. People were so mad that we had to do an impromptu autograph session for the children so that their parents didn't slash the tires of our minivan, or break into the glove compartment to steal the copious amounts of dope that provided the fuel for our theatrical tour. We were so confused by the whole thing that we weren't sure whether to sign our own names or the names of our characters. I would have loved to see the looks on the children's faces when they got their autographed posters home and read the name Samantha Bee. Talk about lunch-bag letdown.

It did, however, give me a chance to meet my ultimate fan. He wrote me a thirty-two-page love letter, and had fashioned himself a custom papier-mâché mask in the style of my character's love interest, which he Scotch-taped to his face just prior to meeting me. I believe the letter stated that he was available for "kisses and cuddles" at a time of my choosing, but when he peeled off the heavy, lumpy mask and stared at me menacingly from across the autograph table, I was more inclined to believe that he might like to slice off my head and store it in the trunk of his car.

Unfortunately for him, I already had eyes for one of my coworkers, a member of the swing cast for our show who, surprisingly, I ended up marrying. I say surprisingly because, after seeing me perform as this character, it is literally a miracle that Jason loves me. It was the kind of performing that people usually do at the end of their career, on the way down, as they spiral into some kind of substance-abuse problem and their hair starts to fall out in clumps due to stress and a general feeling of failure.

You know that a person truly loves you when they still want to have sex with you even after they've witnessed you struggle to pull on a pair of panty hose that is too small for you. Especially if you're engaged in that battle under a makeshift tarp in a Northern Ontario pumpkin patch, while toddlers scream your character's name and their toothless parents hurl cheese curds at the stage to get you to come out.

To be fair, Jason was a member of the B cast and I was the "star" of the A cast, so in our lame hierarchy, I was his superior and could have simply *commanded* him to love me. And his version of Tuxedo Man could not have been more lackadaisical. His job was to seek out the children in the audience with pressing questions for Sailor Moon, and to make sure he held the microphone in the right place so that everyone could hear the child's adorable question.

But he had no patience for two-year-olds and could not abide the lengthy pauses they would take, how much mucus they would smear on the equipment, how many of them would simply breathe loudly into the mic, or burst into tears, totally awestruck by me in my fluorescent ponytail wig. The parents would call him over and he would barrel through the crowd in his big Dracula cape and spats, with his scary top hat and mask, and shove the microphone into the child's face. The children were terrified, the parents were furious, and Jason could not have been more in Heaven.

"Do you have a question for Sailor Moon?"

Silence, as the child looked him over, trembling.

"*Do you* have a question for Sailor Moon?"

Shaking the head, no.

"Well, why did you call me over here if you don't have a question? Maybe someone else would like to ask a question, and now I've come all the way over here for nothing . . ."

Then the parents would try to prompt the child to ask something, anything.

"Hhh. Umm . . . why did . . . uh . . ."

"*What?*"

"Did you . . . did the . . . did the witch . . . uh . . ."

"*I can't hear you. Nobody can hear you. You need to speak up.*"

By this time, the child would be welling up with tears, so Jason would just make up a question for them.

"This is what I heard. When is Sailor Moon's birthday? Does anyone know when Sailor Moon's birthday is? *June* thirtieth! That's right, June thirtieth! That means she's a Cancer!" Or "Where's Sailor Uranus, Sailor Moon? Sailor Uranus isn't here today! I miss her! Don't you miss Uranus, too?"

All the children would hear was Tuxedo Mask yelling at another child, and then either "Sailor Moon Has Cancer" or the word *anus* over and over again. It was pretty terrible.

Jason and I knew we were destined to fall in love when we got wind of a show that had ripped off *our* colossal rip-off of a show, and we raced to the mall to see it so that we could bitch about it. We'd both had the unfortunate experience of auditioning against the actors who actually voice the cartoon, and had felt mortified, so this was our chance to look down on other people for once.

For what it's worth, their show was about a million times worse than ours. They couldn't even rip off the name that we ourselves had ripped off, so they had to call their show "The *Taylor Moone* Show," about a sexy space sailor named Taylor who fought off an evil witch and had a boyfriend who wore a mask, et cetera. They called him Mosquito Man.

Their outfits were store-bought and lame, and they performed the show on a bunch of empty milk crates that they had lashed together with twine. I think Taylor may have actually been wearing a mop on her head instead of a wig. Chumps! We cringed at the poor slobs who had to perform this piece of garbage day in and day out. Then we went out, promptly got drunk, and sealed the deal.

I had finally found someone who shared my warped values, someone who liked the same things I did, a kindred spirit. Bathed in the refracted light of the dollar-store Imperium Silver Crystal that we tossed around the stage like a hot potato, we were a match forged in mutual shame—the Woodward and Newman of the animated live-action-theater fall festival circuit.

At our wedding, my best girlfriend stated that she knew we were a perfect match because we liked to watch the Olympics together with a big bowl of popcorn and pray for the figure skaters to fall on the ice.

Not fair.

First of all, neither of us is particularly religious, so there's no way we would be praying together. And even if we did, we wouldn't technically have been praying for them to fall. We would simply put in the good word that if they *happened* to fall, watching them land on their bums and spin out spectacularly would be *entertaining* for us. Not the same thing at all.

But she was right about one thing—Jason and I are perfectly matched. If the producers of *Sailor Moon* had taken their jobs as seriously as Bummiella and asked us what our perfect jobs would be, we both would have said: If only there were a television show that we could work on as a team that would allow us to explore our darker sides. That would give us the freedom to be actors for a living, and the license to fuck with people a little bit.

Never underestimate the power of the Imperium Silver Crystal.

when animals attack

There are people who do pets, and people who do not do pets. Sometimes those people mingle their genes by making babies, and you never know where their children will end up on the pet spectrum. In our case, Jason and I have one child who chooses to ignore animals completely, unless confronted, let's say, by our cat, desperate for a bit of attention. And believe me, he would have to be pretty desperate to go anywhere near my daughter. If I turn my head for a second, she gets down to work, pushing him off the table or trying to shove his head inside his torso in an effort to kill him and forever remove the threat that he will "look at her" or "eat her pancake." Her father is similarly protective of his pancakes and highly suspicious of any animal that tries to get at them. The other child is enthralled by the cat and wants to stuff its entire body into his mouth, to be kept safe forever in a protective human boy suit. More like his mother.

I am a pet person, always have been—probably because my mother is a pet person. There's no question that when she dies, all of her many cats and dogs and ponies and turtles and lizards will gather sadly around her, and then eat her corpse. To a normal person, this notion may seem grisly and terrible. But trust me, she will have wanted it that way.

I don't have the kind of single-minded dedication to my pets that my mother has, but then again, her level of devotion is rare indeed. She has always had a special connection to her animals that far exceeded anything she could feel for a mere person. If you've ever seen a dog towing a cart in place of its hind legs and thought, *I wonder who would put a dog through that?*, the answer is, my mother. If she had to change a dog's colostomy bag seven times a day for twelve years, she would do it. She would squeeze clean the anal glands of her cat with one hand, scrub the scum from the fins of a clown fish with the other, and endure the loss of a finger from a twenty-pound snapping turtle that she was trying to rescue from the side of the road, before she would change the diaper of one of her grandchildren. That's not really true. She *would* change the diaper, but she would make a face.

My mother had a Siamese cat named Zenny (short for Zen-Buddha) while I was growing up, who was her kindred spirit. Her "familiar," if you will. Their connection was not unlike a woman and her stalker—that is, if the woman was flattered by the stalker's creepy around-the-clock attention, and encouraged him to worship her and mark her as his cat bride. My mother is the only person who ever heard that urban legend about the woman who smeared peanut butter on her nipples for the cat to lick off, and couldn't figure out what the punch line was.

As soon as my mom would get home from work, Zenny would leap into her arms and they would remain inseparable until morning. He would sit on her shoulder and slash at anyone who tried to interact with her. If you had the misfortune of leaving your stuff out, Zenny would urinate all over it just to let you know who was in charge. And if you got on his nerves, he would leave a tiny little turd in your shoe.

My mother thought it was hilarious: "Oh, Zen-Buddha! You're so spirited!" Then they would sort of French each other and go look through a box of sepia-toned photographs of themselves in old-timey costumes.

I walked into the kitchen one day as my mother was draping garbage bags over the mini ceramic barrels that housed all of our kitchen utensils. "I'm tired of Zen-Buddha spraying all our spatulas," she explained.

I looked up at him sitting on my mother's shoulder, and noted how difficult it is, even for animals, to look smug when their eyes are crossed. I wondered aloud if there was any other family on Earth who would tolerate such a thing from an animal.

"Don't be ridiculous. Zenny's part of the family. If *you* peed on all the spatulas, I wouldn't have *you* euthanized."

I wasn't so sure about that.

Zenny just glared at me with his fucky eyes, like he wished *he* could be the one to stick the needle in my neck and depress the plunger himself when the time came. I should have considered myself lucky that he didn't have opposable thumbs; although if there had been a way for my mother to take mine and have them grafted onto his paws, she surely would have. My mother's love for Zenny may have pushed the boundaries of what should comprise a healthy human-pet relationship, but I had to admit that it made me kind of jealous. I wanted a pet to adore me, and I wanted someone else to have to go to school reeking of cat pee, just as I did on an almost daily basis.

When I was about three, my grandmother allowed me to keep a terrarium full of white mice in the basement, even though they horrified and appalled her. I don't know where they came from or who blackmailed her into allowing them in the house, but she must have done something really bad to someone. After all, we are talking about the woman who hated rodents (flying rodents, in particular) so much that she threw herself down a flight of stairs to kill the bat she mistakenly thought had landed in her hair. I guess she was hoping that by bashing her own brains in on the stairs, she would end up crushing the bat in the process. Good thinking.

Wherever the mice came from, I'm positive that I never had a thing to do with their health or care. I certainly never fed them or changed their bedding or visited them or anything—until they started reproducing, at which point I would practically snatch those babies out of their mother's uterus for unlimited loving squeezes. The moment I left the room, the mother mouse must have sighed, looked down at her beautiful mouse babies, and gotten down to the business of eating them all to rid their bald little bodies of the stench of toddler.

Like Lennie from *Of Mice and Men,* I inappropriately caressed every animal I could get my grubby little hands on. I pulled my googly-eyed fish out of their tank to make out with them, popped dog snouts into my mouth without warning, snuggled with worms, and would try to lick your kitten clean like a mother cat if you left me alone with it for more than one second. Many times a person would walk back into the room only to find me with their pet's tiny head jammed into my mouth. I loved the feeling of their quivering eyeballs against the inside of my cheek.

But it was when I moved into my mother's house full-time at the age of eight that the cavalcade of animals really began. She was so occupied with Zenny and his increasing range of needs that she thought it would be helpful for me to take responsibility for some pets of my own. We started simply, with gerbils. I had a male and a female that I named Pierrepont and Pierrepod, respectively. They didn't play, they didn't frolic, they never produced any heirs for me to fuss over and slather with my human juices. They didn't do much of anything, really, except cower from me when I came into the room. Who could blame them? Even *they* probably knew that the touch of a child's hand goes from "embrace" to "crushing death grip" in a split second.

Once I realized that they weren't going to be sleeping in my bed or performing the tricks I tried to teach them anytime soon, I pretty much left them alone. Occasionally, my mother would march up from the basement and report that they had been stewing in their own feces for too long and tell me to clean out the tank. Then she and Zenny would eat from opposite ends of a spaghetti noodle until their mouths united in a tender kiss.

I don't remember being gerbil-less until my early teens, and yet I didn't care much for any of them. They weren't really doing it for me. Whenever one of them would die, I simply renamed his or her replacement Pierrepont or Pierre-pod, depending on whichever sex I assumed it to be, and left them alone to wallow in their own filth and pray for either a water change or a quick death.

Incidentally, I fully acknowledge that I am fated to return to this Earth in the form of gerbil after gerbil, until I have atoned for all these sins. I pray every day that God isn't just a giant gerbil in the sky, or that our extraterrestrial neighbors aren't really a super-intelligent race of space-gerbils looking for the signs of compassion in humankind that will dissuade them from killing us so that they can steal all our sesame seeds and lettuce. Otherwise, I'm in big trouble.

In any case, I soon figured out that guinea pigs were equally deserving of my love and attention. So in addition to my neglected gerbils, my mother bought me a male-female duo of guinea pigs that I charmingly named Stan and Jezebel. Stan was something of a ladies' man. He was basically like a thrusting penis on legs. It took him about half a day to rape Jezebel to death and then continue to rape her unmoving body until we removed her and replaced her with a new, *larger* Jezebel to murder with his penis, which he did immediately. He was a psychopath. It took about seven or eight Jezebels before I figured out his game. I sort of hoped that each new guinea pig couldn't smell the slaughter that had preceded them, but I threw them in regardless.

After a long stare-down, I determined that having such a horny pet was making it impossible for me to love him. I let him go in the basement in the hopes that he would be dispatched instantly by Zenny. I thought it might be fun for him to experience the heart-stopping action that only a cat could provide, and I figured that at least his last moments would be as exciting as the final breaths taken by all of his guinea pig wives. It's possible that he made his way to the sewer system, where he probably banged the entire rat population to death, but I never saw Stan again.

When we moved, my mother let me get my own cat. I still had my gerbils, of course, and Pierrepont and Pierrepod 9.0 were doing great! I had left them by themselves for so long that I had to give them physiotherapy to loosen their atrophied leg muscles. That way they could at least run from one side of the tank to the other in terror as my new cat Gerald stalked them.

Gerald was a great cat. He did all the things that Zenny did, but in a nice way, and was the first in a long line of assorted cats that came and went, each one getting run over by a car or snatched by a hawk or whatever happens to cats when they leave the house and never come back. Gerald nicely complemented the litter of raccoons that the chimney sweep had found living in our house. He was very maternal toward them, but it wasn't until his stomach goiter eventually erupted into a litter of babies that we realized that "he" was a "she." She was a good mom, too, happily nursing the raccoon babies in addition to her own kittens. The "happily" part lasted for about three days, until the raccoon babies started growing insanely fast and making demands that no teat could keep up with.

Raccoons in the house are cute at first. Then their nimble fingers start to annoy you with their amazing capacity to shred your clothes and drapes and intricately dismantle everything of value in your home, such as your stereo equipment and your grandmother's antique charm bracelet. After a while, when they tried to nurse, Gerald and her besieged nipples would run and hide in the attic until they gave up looking for her. When they couldn't nurse, they got mad and tore open every box of crackers and bag of flour in the pantry. In baby raccoon chirps, they mocked us for trying to keep a lid on our kitchen garbage can, and spent the night crunching through chicken bones and munching on maxi pads, scattering trash all over the kitchen floor and falling asleep in a snoring heap under the piano.

As they mature, which they seem to do in about eleven days, raccoons get even more surly and conveniently forget that you rescued them from the burlap sack that the chimney sweep was going to drown them in, and they just go ahead and start trying to kill you. Well, first they threaten the lives of all the other pets, and then they move on to you. There's nothing quite like getting up in the middle of the night to pee and finding a fifteen-pound baby raccoon drinking out of the toilet, who really doesn't appreciate the disturbance, thank you very much. They were the only pets that failed to adequately appreciate all that we had done for them, and never were able to forge a bond with us as a family.

I know that all the experts would say, "They're *wild* animals. That means they're *wild*. They cannot be made into house pets." But we were sure that we had pet-taming superpowers. We knew in our hearts that we were a family of Beast-Masters and that if we had enough time, we could somehow teach ourselves the basics of the raccoon language. So far, we felt confident that we knew when the raccoons were telling us to fuck off, which was pretty much around-the-clock.

One day, I got home from school and they were gone. Just gone. None of us ever spoke about them again. We could have pretended that we were sad, but none of us were that good at acting.

Eventually my mother moved on to livestock. She had always wanted to live in the country, so she moved to a nonworking farm in the middle of nowhere to raise dogs, goats, geese, chickens, guinea hens, and horses. Each animal was more hostile than the next, and my mother was the only one they would tolerate. I was beginning to see a pattern emerging.

The goats would eat the shoes and socks off your feet if you stood still for more than a minute. The geese would attack you with their beaks and wings until you retreated to the safety of your car to wait for someone to rescue you. Even her adorable miniature roosters would fly at your head with their talons outstretched and aimed squarely at your eyes. Her main horse would routinely try to squash you against the wall if you came into the barn without my mother to shield you.

"Oh, you're *exaggerating*. Benson doesn't *hate* you. He's just trying to scratch his back on the wall and you happen to be in the way."

I would look over at him and he'd be innocently munching a carrot like a thousand-pound bunny rabbit. If his horse lips could have formed a sly smile, they would have. And then my mother would stare at me disapprovingly, as she hand-scraped the gook off of his giant horse penis, and say, "Change your shirt, would you? It's filthy. Besides, Benson is afraid of polka dots, and I don't want you spooking him."

She always took his side.

A local woman had half her face bitten off by her horse while trying to feed him carrots from her own mouth. My mother tried to justify it, but we all knew better. "They don't know their own strength. They can really only see peripherally, so he wasn't able to accurately judge the distance to her mouth. That's why it happened." She was extra careful to approach Benson from the side with the carrot in her mouth, so that he could more accurately judge the distance to her mouth.

Her boyfriend, Stewart, was grossed out. "Maybe she shouldn't have been trying to neck with her pet horse in the first place."

"Well, I hardly think she was trying to *neck* with him . . ."

"She should stick some sugar cubes down her blouse next time and see how things turn out." He was desperate to send Benson to the cat-food factory.

"In *France,* people actually *eat horses* . . . the horses don't eat the people."

"You know something? You're sick."

Whenever my mother would leave the vicinity, Benson would instantly flare his nostrils at you and start pawing the ground like an angry bull. It was obvious that he wanted nothing more than to crash through his wooden pen and crush your head with his gigantic horse clogs.

Benson had identified my mother's boyfriend as the number one enemy on his shit list. In an event known from that day forward as Hell Ride, Benson took Stewart, who was innocently trying to exercise him and learn a little more about horseback riding, on a journey to and from the precipice of death. As Benson tore across the property, he made sure that he rubbed Stewart against every tree trunk and every section of fence to try and scrape him off his back. He would fill his lungs with air and then expel it all in a sudden burst, in the hopes that he could dislodge the saddle and the terrified rider, who was clinging to it with all of his strength, as he galloped full speed under low tree branches, and periodically reared. We all got the message about whom Benson really belonged to.

My mother had quite a menagerie on her hands. There were so many cats that she started to name them solely for their identifying physical characteristics. Brown Cat, Spotty Cat, Cat Head, Cat with Stripes, Mean Cat. They all had goopy, pus-encrusted eyes and most of them were pretty mean, so Mean Cat was not to be trifled with. Same with Pus Cat. Since all of the cats fornicated and reproduced with abandon, there were kittens everywhere all the time. Kittens in the barn, kittens in the wood pile, kittens living in a tire swing, kittens in your purse. There were so many kittens that you had to check your boots before putting your feet into them, the way that you have to check your shoes for spiders when you're camping. My mother gave away kittens like some people give away zucchini and tomatoes at the end of a particularly abundant harvest.

"Oh, leaving so soon? Take a bucket of kittens with you for the car . . ."

It wasn't until I became an adult and watched Newton being born that I began to understand her relationship with her pets. It was Thanksgiving 1990, and Orange Cat plopped herself right in front of the stove, where the turkey was roasting, and squirted out more kittens for us to gingerly step around. No one wanted to try to move her, because she would try to climb your body and attack your face and eyeballs if you got in her way.

I named one of her babies Newton and took him home with me. Newton was a real badass, playful and charming and devilish. I was delighted by all of the impish things he would do to annoy other people, like steal the salami out of their sandwich and run away with it, or open the fridge door and eat the entire roast chicken that my roommate had cooked the day before. Adorable.

We had a pretty special relationship. Oh, I had other assorted cats and lizards at the same time, because I was practicing at being a complete social outcast, but Newton was my "special guy." Apparently, he thought I was his "special gal," too, because one night he tried to seal the deal and consummate our love. He wanted to give me the greatest gift of all. The gift of carrying his kittens.

It's horrible when animals try to have sex with you. It's horrible when animals have sex with *each other*, let alone with you. I mean, everybody's got a cute story about so-and-so's dog, who liked to hump your leg when you came over for a barbecue, and how he wouldn't let go until his little lipstick came out of the tube. But that's just child's play, kids' stuff. If you've ever had an animal attack you with intent, then you know exactly what I'm talking about. It's like how everyone says they've had food poisoning, until one day they actually get it, and they go, "Ooohhh. So *that's* food poisoning. Ooooohhh. What I had before was just a cramp."

All you have to do is look at animals doing it to each other to be able to extrapolate. And I do mean doing it *to* each other. It's kind of difficult to tell whether they're trying to copulate or just kill each other, but there is most certainly severe distress involved at every stage. Especially in the feline world. The female cats walk around wailing and carrying on in agony while they're in heat, and then when a male cat obliges, things just seem to go from bad to worse. They climb all over the poor female cat, and she's screaming and trying to get away and looking at you like, *Are you going to just stand there?* Then the male cat bites her neck and pins her down and she just stares off into space, thinking about *The Queen* or something. When he's done he extracts himself from her and licks his testicles clean for about three hours straight, like they're just throbbing with pain. Then she goes off to try and find another cat with better cat semen. It's like the sex scene from *Rosemary's Baby* replaying in a constant loop.

It's the same with every animal.

I have often heard that dolphins are among the only creatures that have sex for pleasure—like, as in a leisure activity. I have also heard them referred to as "the rapists of the deep." I have even heard stories of male dolphins trying to insert themselves into human divers, which I found hilarious for many years. It wasn't until my own incident that I rethought my position on human-dolphin interaction and realized that if a giant fishlike creature tried to rape me, I would drown on the spot. After what Jason and I witnessed, I now think of them as "the *leisurely* rapists of the deep."

Jason and I personally witnessed dolphin-on-dolphin intercourse at an aquarium in Mexico. It was dark and we were the last people there, romantically winding our way through the dolphin enclosures on our way out. There were about six dolphins in one of the big pools, and we noticed that there was quite a flurry of activity below the bridge we were crossing. One of them had a massive erection sticking out of his dolphin body. Let me tell you, you don't notice their smiley faces as much when one of their giant schlongs is staring you in the face. He was chasing one of the other dolphins as she raced madly around in circles. After a few moments, we noticed that she seemed to be wishing that she could grow a set of legs, jump out of the pool, and run away.

I started yelling at the other dolphins. "Help her! Your friend needs help! Help! No! Stop that! *No!* Make him stop, Jason!"

He just looked at me like I had a narwhal tusk growing out of my forehead. "Are you seriously expecting me to jump off this bridge and restrain an erect dolphin?"

I wanted the other dolphins to intervene the way I imagined they would if I was ever being attacked by a shark. Dolphins were like my shark-attack safety net; I thought I could count on them! Nothing. We yelled at the staff in our broken Spanish: *"Ayuda! Por favor! El delfin con . . . sexo!"*

But they just ignored us. Obviously, they saw this all the time, but we were traumatized.

Then, all at once, the remaining dolphins in the pen slowly formed a line and turned their backs on the action, to give the "rapist" dolphin and his victim a little more privacy, I guess. What followed was not pretty. There was a lot of thrashing and dolphin fighting, but mostly just queasiness on the part of the two sunburned people on the bridge in their Señor Frogs T-shirts and fanny packs. I *know* they're not technically fish, but they look enough like fish for me to know that fish sex is just gross.

Anyway, Newton and I had a great relationship. It was everything I had envied about my mother's relationship with Zenny. He didn't ride around on my shoulders, but we still did pretty much everything together. He was a little bit like a dog in the way that he followed me around the apartment and begged for food. My dates and boyfriends found our relationship creepy and threatening, but that's probably only because I referred to him as "my boycatfriend" and, in fact, *was* quite creepy about it. I thought it was cute! We played this little clapping game, where I'd clap at him and squeal, then I'd chase him to one end of the apartment, and then I'd clap at him and squeal, and he'd chase me to the other end of the apartment. We were inseparable.

He was a young cat, unneutered at the time of the incident. I hadn't realized that the attention I lavished on him was making it difficult for him to process the boundaries of our relationship. I didn't know that his burgeoning love for me would one day demand actualization, or that it would happen on my futon on the precise night that I had broken up with my boyfriend, after I realized that he had been streaking snot on the wall behind my couch the entire time we had been dating. Newton would never have done that.

As I settled into my bed, which was only a few inches off the floor on a low wooden frame, I noticed that Newton was sitting in the door frame staring at me. I called him over with my usual cat-call, but he didn't respond. He just continued staring at me, and he looked a little frazzled. His eyes were kind of red-rimmed, and his coat was a bit rumpled, which was unusual, because normally he was quite foppish. I called him over again, but he didn't come.

I didn't think too much of it, until he started emitting this long, low howl and continued staring at me. I was getting a little worried about him; it seemed like he was losing his cat-mind. I'd had plenty of cats in the past that would just wake up one morning and from that day forward only walk in circles, or lick themselves a bald patch or what have you. I thought that was happening to Newton, so I started to get up to go over to him.

Suddenly, he ran at me, screaming. He launched himself at me and somehow attached himself to the back of my skull with his teeth and claws. Like, really *attached* himself. He was screaming, and then I started screaming as I tried to pry his claws out of my head without hurting his tiny paws. But after a while I was like, "Fuck it," and would have pried him off with a crowbar or a shovel if I'd had one, because my scalp was bleeding, and my cat was trying to impregnate my head. And he was really going for it, too, howling and humping my head and holding on for dear life.

It was so confusing for me, because at first I thought he was attacking me, and then I thought, *No, he's trying to make sweet, sweet cat love to me, and this is just what it feels like for female cats.* Then I thought, *Well, one thing I know is that I can never tell another living soul about this because this literally makes me a total loser. It's Saturday night, I just broke up with my boyfriend, I basically sleep on the floor, and my cat is currently fucking me.*

Bleeding, I managed to pull him off and fling him across the room into the doorway, where he resumed staring at me and howling. This time I braced myself and was ready for the next round. He came at me, and I managed to block my head and face, which was no easy feat. I tried to avoid his claws, but it was impossible, and he eventually got ahold of my right arm, which he promptly dug himself into and fiercely bit. He was attached to my arm by teeth and claw, and started to vigorously fornicate with it. I could feel his tiny cat penis trying to poke a hole in my forearm. It took all of my strength to pry him off, and when I did, this time, I threw him against the wall to send a strong message. I was like Jennifer Lopez. I'd had *enough*.

I didn't know how to feel. Was it flattering, on a cat level? On a human level, it was obviously humiliating and shameful, but if I tried to see it from his point of view, was he giving me a compliment of sorts? Was this just courtship? Were we going steady now? Also, I considered the possibility that I had brought it upon myself. With all of my Beast-Master magical animal intuitiveness, had I mistakenly sent a message that I was somehow available?

After a third and fourth attack, I no longer cared. I was bleeding, disheveled, and covered in a sticky substance that I had to assume was cat semen. I checked my head and made an appointment to have his testicles removed posthaste.

I spent many months wondering what the "take away" was, but in the end, it was *so* obvious. It wasn't that I was a sad and lonely woman, a living embodiment of the "crazy cat lady" stereotype, who badly needed to get out of the house and start making some human friends. Not at all! Quite the contrary! This was an accomplishment of the highest order. I had done it! I had outshone even my mother with my command over the animal kingdom. She was going to be *so jealous.*

To this day, I occasionally catch myself sharing a secret smile with the odd cat or two, as if to say, "I may need to call on you someday—await my signal." They look at me for a bit, and then turn away as if they're too intimidated to hold my gaze. Then they run off and lick their testicles clean for an hour or so. I have to assume that it's because they find me so attractive. Now that's what I call power.

gurr-bulls

Jason and I were looking at old photographs the other day and came across one that makes my heart skip a beat every time I see it. It is a photo of a person of indeterminate age and gender on horseback, the horse standing astride a row of plump harvest pumpkins, and a girl with her back turned, standing beside the horse and comfortably holding on to its bridle. I recognized the horse; of course, it was one of my mother's, a handsome gelding named CG. The person in the saddle is sporting a hideous pair of flaming orange cotton tights, an oversize purple sweatshirt with a belt, and a plain, boyish haircut. The young girl standing beside the horse has clearly returned from an invigorating ride, her jodhpurs and boots are dusty and well worn, and her long brown hair is gathered into an unruly ponytail at the base of her neck.

"Ugh . . . I hate this picture," I said, as I tried to snatch it away from Jason.

"Why? You look so good in it! I love this one."

"What are you talking about? I look awful. I hate my hair in this picture. I can't believe anyone would let me out of the house in those tights . . ."

He grabbed the photo and stared at it in horror.

"Wait a minute—that's *you? On the horse?* Oh-my-God—I thought you were the *other one.* I thought this was a picture of you taking a mentally disabled child out for a therapeutic horseback ride . . ."

All those years, Jason had thought that I was the attractive, mysterious stranger in the photo, not the amorphous blob staring blankly into the camera. My pulse started racing like I'd been caught in a lie, but on the surface I tried to brush it off like it was no big deal.

"Well, I don't really think it's anything to get *too* upset about—"

"I've gotta think about this. Oh, man. Whoa. What the hell—"

"Yeah, but things are different now. I mean, you love me *now,* right? We all have times in our lives that we'd like to forget about. It's not like you look so attractive in your prom picture, you know . . ."

"Jason from the prom picture would never have dated Samantha the Make-A-Wish child in the orange tights."

"Okay, but what about Jason, proud recipient of a 'participation' certificate for 'Satisfactory Achievement in Middle School Square Dancing'? The one with the acne issues and the difficult-to-maintain side hair part?"

"That guy is *infinitely* more fuckable than this girl. This picture is so bad it's making me question my life choices right now. *Oh,* my *God*—what do I do whatdoIdowhatdoIdo . . . ?"

He was looking around the room like a caged animal. I thought he might try to claw his way out through the screen door like a raccoon that gets down your chimney and ends up trapped in your house by accident. I've always suspected that one day the jig would be up. Here we have Jason, so handsome and photogenic, and his wife, by all photographic accounts homely, and, in this case, of indecipherable gender. I'm well aware that I only look acceptably good when conditions are optimal— hair blown dry, a light dusting of makeup, discreet girdle in place—but pull one block out of that Jenga pile and the whole thing collapses. Catch me fresh out of the shower and you'll know what I'm talking about. In walks Samantha Bee, and out walks Aileen Wuornos, hair wetly slicked back, ready to shiv you with a sharpened spoon in the lavatory of the ladies' penitentiary. One day, a few years from now, my current face is going to fall off, and from that point forward Jason will have to push our twin beds apart for good. And I will have no right to blame him for that.

This particular photograph is so perfectly representative of where I was as a woman circa 1990, in my third year of college. It was taken smack in the middle of the most forgettable of all of my dramatic image makeovers. I had gone from "intriguing junior" to "sexually ambivalent career cafeteria worker" in just under three bad haircuts. I had allowed myself to become an experimental hair model for a local hairdresser who clearly had a thing for eleven-year-old boys. Every time I went to him, my hair got shorter and shorter, while the sideburn area grew longer and longer. But, as a side benefit, my hymen started to regenerate itself, thicker and more virginal than ever, purely from lack of use.

At the time, my best friend Meredith and I were living in a huge two-bedroom apartment off campus, and we were into things like "angrily discussing American Imperialism" and "vegetarian cookery." Although we both still secretly loved meat and could easily snake down a whole coil of contraband kielbasa when the other person wasn't home, publicly we refused to eat it, preferring instead to simply substitute cheese in its place. No longer comfortable in normal pants, we favored anything with an elasticized waistband to accommodate our ever-expanding waistlines.

We liked to spend our days dyeing our hair purple in the sink, bleaching our mustaches, and accumulating cats. We had four between us. You couldn't take a step into our apartment without getting kitty litter embedded in your foot, which was one of the reasons nobody ever came over, but certainly not the only one. We read each other's tarot cards all the time and consulted a Ouija board for the big decisions, and always tried to conjure the presence of Jack the Ripper at the last minute to spice things up a bit. Also, as I recall, we had numerous dream catchers and a "kitchen witch."

Although it would have surprised any onlooker to know

that both of us weren't virgins, one of us actually was. I was glad it wasn't me, but it hardly put me in a position of social superiority. Active in high school and early on in college, I had decided to put my sexuality on hold for a while, or rather, my haircut had made that decision for me, while my fashion sense came up the rear to cinch the deal. I favored colorful tights to draw the most attention possible to my leg and haunch area, with big, thick-belted T-shirts and combat boots to complete the androgyny.

Due to the plentiful cat fur that coated every square inch of our apartment, all of our clothing was saturated with enough dander to immediately asphyxiate the cat allergic. There was a girl in one of my theater classes whose face would swell up every time I walked past her wearing one of my signature chunky knits.

Neither of us ever wore makeup, because although we claimed that we didn't want to feed the "beauty industry beast," really, neither of us actually knew how to put it on. And if and when we did, we just looked like Debra Winger at the end of *Terms of Endearment* when she's dying and she's trying to put on a brave face for her children.

Meredith and I lived very happily for a long time in that apartment; we were like the two batty old crones on the block that all the neighborhood children would run from and accuse of being witches. But eventually money got tight, and we thought it might be time to add a roommate, just to smooth things out financially. We decided that getting a girl would be too weird; she might feel like a third wheel because we were so bonded, and we didn't need to change the dynamic that was obviously working so well for us. It had to be a guy.

We put an ad in the college paper and dudes started showing up at our apartment, but there were no takers. We never considered the possibility that *we* were the weirdos, and that every guy who stepped into our space might feel like he was entering the *What Ever Happened to Baby Jane?* house, population: two Baby Janes on the hunt for a roomie. We laughed and laughed at the men who toured the apartment. This one had dead eyes, that one had bad juju. We burned sweetgrass every time one of them left, to get rid of all their hostile energy. We never stopped to think that the moment they walked into the living room and saw me hand-feeding my pet lizard cat food from a plastic spoon, they might have gotten spooked and run for their lives.

That is, until Ryan entered the picture.

He knocked at the door and Meredith answered it. I could hear her talking to him through the screen, and right away I knew that this one was going to be different. Her voice had gotten so small and girly, it sounded like potpourri was sprinkling out of her mouth and scattering on the floor tiles. As Meredith floated up the stairs to our apartment, she looked right through me. I could tell that she was wishing me physical harm. That she just knew that I was going to fail whatever test Ryan was going to put us through before deciding whether or not he wanted to live with us, and she pre-hated me for it.

He was a real specimen. About six foot something, tanned, muscular, attractive . . . great hair, well-worn clothes that made him look outdoorsy and sexily disheveled.

"Hey, I'm Ryan."

He grabbed my hand and held it firmly in his. I played it cool, but out of the corner of my eye I could tell that our handshake was already driving Meredith mental. I could see her suppressing the urge to pee on him to claim him definitively as her own.

As she showed him the apartment, it was like a different person was inhabiting her body. Her laughter got so loud and giddy it annoyed both me *and* my lizard, Otis, who was sitting on the floor beside me as I fed him cat food from a plastic spoon. But Ryan was unfazed. Miraculously, he liked our place and didn't seem to mind the menagerie of animals that inhabited every nook and cranny of the apartment. Having grown weary of slaying women everywhere he went, I'm sure that the possibility of living with the antithesis of female sexuality would feel like a refreshing change of pace.

"I hope you don't mind. I'm teaching myself to play the guitar. I'll try to keep quiet with it. I'm kind of a night owl."

Guitar. He played the *guitar*.

"And is it cool if I chain my kayak to the shed in the backyard? I like to take her out on weekends, so I don't want to have to put her in storage if I don't have to . . ."

If you never thought you could hear the sound of two women simultaneously ovulate before, you could that day.

Just a little "pop," a little disturbance in the force, and it was over.

On the glorious day that he moved in, Meredith and I put our little twin beds into a room together, like eight-year-old sisters. Nothing was going on in our beds anyway, so what did it really matter? It would just give us more time to giggle ourselves to sleep and challenge each other with Marry-Eff-Kill scenarios until the wee hours of the morning. Of course, all we really wanted to do was first eff and then marry Ryan, even if we had to kill each other to make it happen.

The first morning that we woke up after Ryan moved in, I found Meredith fluttering around the kitchen wearing red lipstick, humming to herself, and whipping up a frittata. I had never seen such a thing in my life.

"Uh . . . what's going on here?"

"What? *Qué te pasito?*" she said loudly for the benefit of Ryan. "I'm just making a traditional *tortilla,* the food of my native people."

Her Spanish heritage had never come into play before, but Ryan had mentioned some traveling he had done in South America, and so It. Was. *On.*

"I know you *gringas* like to have cereal for breakfast, but I think to myself, *Today iss a new day.* Why are joo dress like that?"

I was going for a run. For the first time in my life.

We glared at each other. I left her playing Suzy Cream-Cheese in the kitchen and ran around the block for five minutes. Having never engaged in any form of physical activity before, I immediately had to return home doubled over with intestinal cramping. My insides weren't used to getting jiggled like that.

Things went on just like that for two weeks, though our contact with Ryan was minimal at best. It had never occurred to us that our new roommate might sleep until 2 p.m. every day, disappear for a while, and then return home well after we were asleep in our beds, exhausted from having peered out the window waiting up for him all night long.

I soured on his unattracted-to-me-ness quickly, and sensed that our apartment was merely destined to be a way station for him, a place for him to store his personal effects and pile up dirty laundry. Although he was gorgeous and dynamic and had smooth skin that appeared to self-tan without any need of sun or chemicals, as time passed I found his personal habits increasingly distressing. It was charming that he was teaching himself guitar at night, but soon the first three bars of "Dust in the Wind" grew tiresome to me and I longed for him to move on to "Smoke on the Water," let's say, or the first six chords of "In-A-Gadda-Da-Vida." A well-known local singer had befriended him in a bar and started giving him music lessons for free. I wondered why he wasn't progressing at all in his lessons, and then realized that their constant porking was probably getting in the way.

He never seemed to shower and would eat *anything*—two things that conspired to make him extra smelly. *I* was convinced that I detected a faint scent of kippers behind him everywhere he went, whereas Meredith preferred to think of him as just simply "woodsy." He got all of his groceries at a secondhand store that stockpiled only previously rejected canned goods, so our cupboards were full of dented tins of smoked oysters and various potted meats. I came home many times to find the burnt and reeky residue from his preferred dish, a stewy mung of canned fish, bamboo shoots, and creamed corn, clinging to the bottom of one of my precious pots. He had left it behind confident in the knowledge that someone else, for example, me, would clean it up. Hadn't he noticed the charming sign I had posted above the light switch that read KITCHEN'S CLOSED: THIS CHICK'S EGGS-AUSTED with the picture of the tired-looking chicken wiping her sweaty brow? Needless to say, the kitchen witch was not impressed.

I noticed that he had a fan base of other dowdy women who followed his every move and ensured that he was fed and well cared for and that his assignments were typed, which was a huge turn-off for me. I was forever taking messages from them and could feel their seething hatred through the phone. How dare I live with him? Use the same toilet seat as him? Inhabit the same apartment space as he cleaned his taut body in the shower? I hated to inform them that that was a bimonthly occurrence at best.

"Just tell Ryan that Anneliese called. The poetry jam has been moved to Yuki's apartment . . . no need to bring chips, I've got lots. Make sure you tell him that. He doesn't need to bring any snacks."

"So, no chips . . . got it."

"It's Anneliese. A-N-N-E—"

"Got it."

"*Do* you? *Do* you '*got*' *it*?"

I could tell that she was imagining me as a much more physically attractive person than I actually was.

"Sorry, I'm just so busy and scatterbrained! I totally forgot I'm supposed to shave Ryan's balls tonight—I don't know if he's going to be able to make your gay poetry jam after all!"

It was time for him to get his own phone line.

When he brought a girl home, Meredith and I would tiptoe out of our shared room and grab two glasses so that we could listen to them doing it through the wall. We tittered to each other and pretended that we found it icky and gross, but then after a while we would just get quiet and retreat to our single beds for some lonely introspection. The next day we were always curt with him, and would try to sting him with a well-placed barb: "Get much *sleep* last night, Ryan? Because *we* didn't. Sure was a lot of noise in the apartment last night." "Wow. I'm just *exhausted* this morning, aren't *you*, Meredith? Something really *loud* must have *kept me awake all night*." "How did your *guitar lesson* go? Get any new *fingering techniques* you'd like to share with the class?"

We could not have been more annoying. If he noticed, he never seemed to show it, and would just end up working off his hangover on the couch, watching a *Gremlins* marathon all day on television.

"How do you figure they got those *gurr-bulls* to act so good?"

SAMANTHA BEE

I didn't even begin to know how to deconstruct that sentence. I waited for him to start laughing at his own joke, but the laugh never came.

"You realize that the movie is called *Gremlins*, right? *The movie is about gremlins*."

He nodded dully. "Oh, right. Yeah. Of course."

"There's no such thing as a gurr-bull . . . it's *gerbil*. And they look nothing like that. They're like mice. They also don't usually transform into demons when you throw water on them . . . so . . ."

"I wonder how they get those *gremlins* to act so good . . ."

Meredith didn't seem bothered by his presence at all. One day she came home with a blond streak in her dark hair. The next, she had joined the Peace Corps. Anything to get Ryan's attention and keep it long enough to have a conversation, which would usually max out at five minutes. She made canapés, she made tapas, she painted her toenails; it started to make me feel sad that she cared so much what he thought, when he never really thought of either of us at all.

In my imagination I had stopped caring that he wasn't into me, and started disliking him for not being into my friend, whom I loved. I was desperate for her to realize how little there was beneath his chiseled surface, and I secretly hoped that his penis was as tiny as his hands were large and manly and impressive. I had begun to see how he never got anything right and didn't know anything at all about pop culture, a crime which I found unforgivable.

The chickens in his henhouse would all gather around

him and he'd start to tell some dumb story about something
he saw on television when he was eight and how it had im-
pacted his life forever.

"Remember that show *That's Amazing*?"

"Are you referring to the show *That's Incredib*—"

"Yeah. *That's AMAZING*. What a show . . . what a show.
I'll never forget the story of this one man—it was incredible."

I grabbed Meredith's shoulder and whispered, "Oh. My.
God."

He spoke so slowly and deliberately, like he was preparing to impart some mystical droplet of wisdom on us. Everyone was rapt.

"They had this waiter once who could remember, like,
everything everyone ordered. Like, thirty people's orders.
Without writing it down. To the T."

All the women gasped.

I hissed at Meredith, "First of all, it's 'to *a* T.' And the
show was called *That's Incredible!* Fran Tarkenton hosted it.
Don't you remember? And the guy from—"

"Shhh! You're being *so rude. Quit being such a bitch!*"

He then went on to list every food item that the waiter
had been required to remember, as if he remembered it accurately from when he had watched the show as a child. I
could smell the women's pheromones leaking out from their
lymph nodes and wafting over to him as he captivated them
with his miraculous story of "the waiter who could remember things."

"—strawberry ice cream. A cheeseburger with the works and a Coke. Two fish tacos and a side of guacamole. Piggies in a blanket—"

Ryan had this terrible habit of letting our cats out of the apartment, too. He was just so oblivious to their presence and had his head so high up in the oxygen-starved atmosphere that it never occurred to him to look down when opening or shutting the door. For some reason our cats were always bolting for the outdoors. Even they were probably sick of us. If anyone but Ryan had let Meredith's most prized cat, King Marmalade, out the door, it would have meant instant banishment. Daggers. Guilt trips for days, complete with the sounds of Meredith sobbing down by the railroad tracks and wailing her cat's name. "Marmie? *Marmoo?* Come *home*! Mummy loves you, *King Marmaloo*! *Special food!*" She would pop open twelve tins of Fancy Feast to tempt her cat with the sound of the vacuum seal releasing.

Eventually, her cat always found its way home. It would spend three or four days eating trash out of a Dumpster and getting worms, and then lurk home looking for some of that rancid horse meat they try to pass off as food for cats. But when *Ryan* let her cat out, which he did about seventy-eleven times, it was cool. The whole time he was home she went about her business like nothing had happened, and then the second he left, she was down by the railroad tracks again holding a candlelight vigil.

One time I caught him dipping the wrong end of the shrimp into the cocktail sauce at a party held in his honor to commemorate something one of his horny friends made up to get him over to her house for the afternoon.

"*Stop!*" I cried. "You're dipping the tail in the sauce!"

"What?" he said densely. "It's edible, isn't it?" I noticed that he didn't seem to have any leftover tails on his cocktail plate. This guy was like a fucking seagull. I'd have to remember to cut all the plastic six-pack soda rings in the house so he didn't choke on one the next time he filter-fed in our apartment. Maybe he was one of those weird people who also ate all the watermelon seeds for the extra crunch. He seemed to be having a lot of trouble identifying very common items on a platter of appetizers, too.

"What the *hell* is this?" he asked, as he carefully observed a pickle that had been hollowed out and stuffed with cream cheese. I would grant him that it did not need to be stuffed with cheese, but all the same, it was obviously a pickle.

"Um. It's a pickle."

He just stared at me. "A *what*?"

"A pickle. A pickled cucumber. Like . . . a *pickle*."

He chuckled a little, like I was trying to get him to eat a plate of unicorn droppings or something.

"Okay, buddy. Whatever you say."

"Yes, *I'm* the crazy one."

Things were always better between us when his mouth was closed.

I was starting to think that he was a drug addict, and I would have gone through his stuff to find out if it hadn't been so stinky and all crumpled into one corner of his room.

SAMANTHA BEE

Every time he was out of my eye line, I'd try to remember what the big deal was about this guy. Why all the fuss? Why all the free passes? And then he'd bolt out of the bathroom to his room after a (rare) hot shower, sans towel, and it would all come back to me in a flash. I'd have to go throw all that pent-up energy into making him a casserole with a side of homemade focaccia.

Even my mom was in love with him a little bit, and she didn't usually go for that kind of guy. She normally reserved her girlish crushes for fellows who were clearly at their peak of attractiveness back in the seventies: guys with big bushy mustaches and mom jeans, or guys on obnoxiously loud "crotch rockets," as she liked to breathlessly say. But she, too, fell under Ryan's spell. Until one day when she brought her horrible dog over for a visit and got a powerful whiff of that irresistible man-musk. We were having a little barbecue and my mom didn't like to go anywhere without her dirty little Jack Russell terrier, Bubbles. Bubbles liked to kill cats. He liked it a *lot*. So whenever he came over, we had this system where we'd tie him to the garden shed in the backyard and he'd yap all day at every butterfly that flew by or every breeze that touched his snout.

My mother had specific instructions for Ryan, because he wasn't used to the protocols surrounding the care of Bubbles, and I had prewarned her that explaining something to him could take a while.

"Whatever you do, *don't* let him off the leash, because he'll run down the street and then I'll have to go catch him!"

She was nervously tittering as she said it, to give the impression that although these minor details were *important,* she was still cool and, you know, *whatever* about it. But the details *were* important. If you ever let him go, Bubbles would run like a bat out of Hell in the opposite direction and not stop until he found a creature only slightly smaller than himself to maul to death.

"If you see that he's out of water or food, please feel free to replenish it, just *don't* let him off the leash, whatever you do. I don't want to have to run after him! Not in *these heels.*" She was trying to keep it light, and yet also draw his eye downward to her impractical but cute footwear. And she didn't want to make him feel too stupid, just in case he somehow might have wanted to give her a sensual massage sometime in the future. But his eyes were not reflecting any understanding whatsoever of the words she was saying to him, and I could tell she was worried.

About fifteen minutes later, Ryan came in from outside and announced to the whole roomful of people, and to no one in particular, "Someone's little dog just ran down the street."

My mother shrieked. "Was it Bubbles? Oh my God! What happened? Where did he go? When did this happen?"

He thought about it. "About fifteen minutes ago."

My mother took off down the street in her tie-up wedge espadrilles shouting the dog's name, but Bubbles was nowhere in sight. Meredith and I listlessly looked for him, hoping that he had been run over by a passing train.

My mother returned, sweaty and disheveled, with only one dirtied espadrille and the dog in her arms, happy as a clam.

"That young man is too simple to pound sand," she said tersely. "Is he *jumbled*?" Which was her politically correct way of asking whether he had previously sustained any kind of brain damage.

When Ryan left us, he did so swiftly and with stealth. He gave us barely any notice, and a check for two months' rent so that we wouldn't have anything to complain about as he packed his single box and rolled up his well-used futon. For him, moving was an effortless afterthought. He was simply answering the call of a better opportunity that had come his way. He was completely unaware that Meredith and I had been fighting over the position of First Wife ever since he moved in, and that in our minds, we had not been getting along with him for months.

The two of us picked up part-time jobs to fill the gap in funds. I conveniently got a job at a women's dress shop I liked to frequent. I called it Ye Olde Fatt Shoppe behind its back, and pretended not to like the clothes for a while, but eventually succumbed to the comfortable allure of its signature cotton dirndls, at a staff discount. After all, who did we have to unsuccessfully try to impress now that our greasy/sexy roommate was gone?

Sadly, we let his room remain empty. Not sad in that forlorn way that parents sometimes maintain their children's old rooms as shrines to their childhoods, but sad in the sense that we were just . . . sad. Because we actually really liked our Lucy and Ricky Ricardo twin-bed arrangement and we didn't want to change it.

I haven't seen or heard from Ryan since, but I know that one day I will just open up a magazine and there he will be. Famous, mostly for doing something marvelous and strange, like flying around the world in a two-seater plane with a blind pilot, crop-dusting various developing nations with rations of dented canned goods and deodorant—a sign that he *had* been listening to me the whole time. That without even realizing it, I had unwittingly been the Bela Karolyi to his Nadia Comaneci, and now he was taking my lesson in good hygiene and paying it forward. And that's all the acknowledgment I—his mentor and coach—could ever hope for.

looking a gift horse in the mouth

I have an affliction that cannot be cured. It affects me annually around the holiday season and at a few other scattered points throughout the year, on people's birthdays. It's an obsession with finding the pitch-perfect gift, accompanied by a severe mental block when it comes to interpreting that person's needs and desires. Like an atrophy of the gift-giving muscle.

I've tried hard all my life to do it right, and years of both missing the mark terribly and being at the receiving end of some of the most thoughtless gift-giving possible have fueled my passion to do better, though it is endlessly tiring. I would be extremely happy if I came from a family that composed original poetry, or pulled names out of a hat to give one single gift as our preferred mode of holiday expression. But in our family, everybody has to get everybody else a present, and that's the way it goes. If you tried to give someone a poem *instead* of a present, you would find yourself on the receiving end of a clusterfuck of confusion, as the person repeatedly tried to dig through the envelope it came in to find the gift card for Best Buy that surely must have dropped out somewhere along the way.

I am cursed by my mother's insistence on using her wits, and my own insistence that a gift should perfectly reflect the recipient's uniqueness. She's always doing things like freezing a road-kill porcupine in order to remove the quills and fashion you a sunglasses case festooned with hand-cut beads. Or knitting a dickie for your cat, or making homemade deodorant for you that comes in a holster she made by tanning her own deerskin. You're never quite sure what to do with these things, but you always feel the love and care that goes into every stitch.

And as one of those people who always search for the most perfect gift to reflect the spirit of every occasion, I have been disappointed time after time by other people's lack of enthusiasm for the ritual. I mean, if you're going to put on a blindfold and feel around the inside of a Dumpster for something you can wrap in the paper I wrapped your last gift with and toss it to me Christmas morning from across the room, maybe you shouldn't bother. I don't need a gift. So you can use your gift-giving impulses to make other people's dreams come true.

I don't want a gift. I repeat, I don't *need* a gift. Honestly. It's more insulting to me that you would wrap the cardigan of a dead person eight sizes larger than me and try to pass it off as something I would wear than if you just said, "We're not doing gifts this year." If you give me a turquoise, size-sixteen, funnel-neck sweatshirt with three-quarter-length sleeves and a relief portrait of rabbits frolicking in the snow, then I know you didn't really want to bother getting me something in the first place. A gift like that reveals what you were thinking when you bought it—namely, *Ugh. I don't know what size she goddamn wears. This one's got rabbits on it. She's a girl. It'll do.* And then you shoved it in a box, wrapped it in last year's Samantha Bee Christmas Color Palette, and didn't even do a proper job of tucking in the corners and nicely taping them down.

Anyway, I got you an original vintage ivory Masatoshi goblin netsuke for your curio cabinet because I thought it was as beautiful and special as you are. I hope you like it.

I can agree in principle that it's the thought that counts when giving or getting gifts, but I would also like to point out that "if there's no thought . . . it doesn't count." I don't wish to be reminded that you didn't want to take the time to get to know me, or perhaps you have even known me my whole life and simply don't care about me. All I ask is that you not rub my face in it.

For example, if you are my boyfriend, you should probably think about giving me something other than a gift certificate to the liquor store for my birthday. If your next impulse is to write me a check for $50 and put it in a Tiffany ring box for me to breathlessly open, that's probably not going to work either. I will take that check for $50, "boyfriend," and I will pay my phone bill with it, thank you very much! Then I will take my liquor store gift card and get massively fucked up on Amarula, then smoke a pack of menthol cigarettes for no reason and make nonsensical phone calls to you at four o'clock in the morning on my phone line that has recently been reinstated.

In my case, the thought simply *has* to count . . . otherwise, it's just going to be confusing for you when you receive your membership to the Bacon of the Month Club, let's say, because of that time five years ago when you mentioned that you had never had the chance to try real Canadian bacon and I never forgot it.

Every year on December 1, I run out and spend about twelve hundred million thousand dollars making the gifts I have bought look like they leapt out of the pages of *Persnickety Old Opera-Loving Gay Man's Quarterly.* So when you fold up my paper and ribbons and try and regift them back to me next year, nice try, but I have a small space carved in my brain dedicated solely to a catalog of wrapping "looks." I practice making new and more voluminous bows every year the way some people practice things like being good parents or caring for elderly relatives. I don't have time for *those* things, but my Christmas memories and monochromatic color schemes are priceless.

So it's highly distressing to me that I am the only person in my life who cares at all about the beautification and perfection of the holiday season. But it's even more distressing for me when people don't care about the gifts I have painstakingly acquired for them. You may not care whether I ever make it through that stale jellybean pile you regifted from your office Secret Santa, but I have been torturing myself to come up with the perfect gift for you for months, and I'd like a little love in return, please.

Because I can tell you that even if you were standing in your backyard one day, and your dog shat out a pair of jodhpurs that would make me look like the bulb of an onion, and you wrapped them in a creosote-soaked blanket and gave them to me on my birthday, I would still make you feel like I had been waiting all my life to own those pants. I would compliment them, and try them on, and rave about them, and take a picture of myself randomly wearing them and send it to you, and you would feel special and precious and well-thanked for your thoughtfulness, even though I would immediately understand that you don't give a rat's ass about me.

I'm sorry. I don't mean to belittle your gift-giving impulses just because I've been burned so often. The truth is that I would fucking *wear* that bullshit turquoise, funnel-neck sweatshirt with the rabbits to *Christmas fucking dinner,* even though I knew that the cameras would be snapping and cherished memories would be documented. That's how much I care about your well-being.

So I really don't like it when I work hard to get people stuff and they open their gifts the way a dog eats a treat, while looking *past* the treat the whole time to see if there is a treat in the other hand, too. I like my gifts to be savored, not swallowed without chewing. Don't look behind my gift to see if there's a better gift on its way, like you're trying to get into a club or something and you've run into some nerd who might hurt your chances.

Let me spell it out for you. Here's how it should work:

See my gift. Yes, you may touch it, I know it looks beautiful. Remark that it is well-wrapped and how you always like my unique take on Christmas and birthday gifts. Slowly begin to unwrap the gift. Maybe try a little "Ooh, I should really save this ribbon/paper, etcetera, for next year!" (Only don't, because I'm not sure you can handle the responsibility.) Now peel back the paper and appear to get excited. Don't overdo it, but let's have a little enthusiasm. Now mull it over a bit, tell me where you think this gift fits into your life, and thank me for it. Then, place it carefully to your side. Don't put it in harm's way, but also, don't be a geek about it. If you lay it on too thick, I'll know that you're just mocking me, and then next year, you're getting a mug filled with Reese's Pieces that I stole from a Walgreens. (I'm just kidding, I could never do that. I hate Reese's Pieces!)

Now, my father knows how to accept a gift. He knows how to accept one mainly because he wrote his wish list in blood on the dining room wall and has been practicing his acceptance speech ever since. It doesn't really bother me, except that every year the gifts keep getting more and more expensive. It makes me feel weird that my own father asks me for stuff he would never have contemplated getting for me while I was growing up. The man who once gave me a budget of $13 a week for groceries in college—that's $52 a month for food—is now asking me for things like laptop computers and Gucci loafers.

One year, I got him an iPod, which he loved and was moved by. I wasn't making so much money that it was an inconsequential expense, but I could afford it with a little stretching. I knew it would mean a lot to him. Two months later, the whole transaction was forgotten. It was all, "This iPod stinks. It only has six hours of battery life! I hate it."

I was like, "Six *hours*? Who can listen to that much Bruce Hornsby in a single day anyway? I mean, maybe if the Range was still in the picture . . . but a solo effort? Don't you need to give your ears time to stop bleeding before you fire that bad boy up again?"

"Bite me. It's a lot better than the Smiths, so get over yourself." He always liked to remind me that I went through a very serious love affair with the music of the Smiths and that he thought it was terrible and depressing. I liked to remind him that Billy Joel was a much more interesting songwriter when he was suffering from depression and doing things like drinking furniture polish, not making songs like "Uptown Girl," which was, coincidentally, my father's favorite.

"Whatever. I need a Nano."

"I'd like to remind you that I was the person who bought you your embarrassingly obsolete iPod two months ago, and that it cost over four hundred dollars, so I'm probably the wrong person to be complaining about this to."

"If I buy a yellow one online, can I use your credit card and then I'll pay you back with a check?" Which was really just code for "Buy me one. Now."

There are many people in this world who do not know how to accept a gift properly. I don't really know if it's part of a Depression-era mentality or having self-esteem issues that makes it impossible for them to imagine that someone would give them a gift from the heart. Perhaps the recipient was raised by wolves or grew up in the base of an old oak tree, and like Nell, communicated using only a primitive, guttural language system that doesn't include such niceties as "Thank you" or "Wow, that sure was thoughtful." In any case, many of those people are related to me by blood and I bear the scars to prove it.

I have learned to stop buying gifts of any kind for people in my family over the age of seventy, for instance. It's just a lose-lose proposition. It really doesn't matter how much effort you put into the present; if they haven't bought it for themselves, they just don't believe that you got it from Sears, and therefore, it just won't do. And they don't care at all about fully disparaging your gift while you sit there next to the Christmas tree, hoping beyond hope to bring a glimmer of sunshine into their lives.

"I hate this," said my grandfather after reluctantly pulling the paper off his gift of a sweater vest and leather slippers. "Will *you* wear it?" he asked, gesturing for me to put it on.

"No, Granddad, I bought it for you. You asked me for a sweater vest, remember?"

"Well, this isn't the one I wanted. The one I wanted was from Sears. This one doesn't even have sleeves! It'll bind me up."

Everything binds old people up. Pajamas, things with or without sleeves, bedsheets . . . you'd think they were spending their off hours rolling around on the floor trying to put out a fire. I would have gotten him socks, but I was afraid he would hang himself with them.

"Can you take it back? I'll never use it. Take the slippers back, too. Those are slippery—I'll get all tangled up in the night on the way to the toilet."

And my grandmother was somehow even worse.

"Dammit! I told you not to get me towels! I have *too many towels*!" she hissed.

"But these ones are so soft and the ones you have in the bathroom are so scratchy! I thought you'd like them! You deserve softness!"

"Just don't get me gifts! Jesus! I *told* you not to. I begged you not to." She was practically in tears.

"I'm so sorry!"

Angry glare. "Just don't let it happen again."

I suppose they had a point. They just didn't want me spending what little money I had on frivolous things when they felt they had everything they needed for the rest of their lives. It didn't really help my case that they had such a skewed notion of what things cost that they could imagine that a set of hand towels would be equal to the cost of a year's college tuition.

My granddad had recently held a garage sale in which he priced everything ludicrously high. A rabbit-ear television set that got two channels in black-and-white had a price tag of $100 on it. A giant brown crocheted owl perched on a stick was priced at $45, and the pièce de résistance, a picnic basket, was priced at $150. *What could possibly be in that picnic basket?* I wondered. When I opened it up, I found a dog-eared copy of *I'm OK, You're OK,* some rusty toenail clippers, a box of douching powder from the 1950s, and some leftover tubing from a home enema kit. It suddenly made sense that they might think a sweater vest from the Gap could be worth a down payment on a house.

It has always been this way, and it has been a hard road. My whole life has been a series of gift misfires, all with the best of intentions. When I was young, throwing money at a gifting opportunity seemed too gauche. Best to make it personal, and funny!

As a little girl, I gave my father a lump of coal for Christmas one year. I wasn't angry with him, I just thought it was a hilarious private joke. I can't remember why I thought it would be funny, I just did. I cleverly figured out where I could acquire a handsome piece of coal, wrapped it carefully in a beautiful box, and waited on pins and needles until the day my joke would see the light of day. When he opened it, he came just shy of bursting into tears of disappointment. He had probably requested some Paco Rabanne or something, and couldn't see that I thought he had such a great sense of humor that he would totally get it, and that in this case, the journey itself was better than the destination.

I once gave my uncle a T-shirt that read I ONLY DRINK ON DAYS THAT END IN Y. I thought it was hilarious when I was ten. And perhaps in retrospect, it wasn't the greatest gift, but I was still laughing when I noticed the hush that befell the entire room once he unwrapped it. It had a picture of a red-nosed boozehound on it, like Andy Capp, and little hiccup bubbles that floated above him. I thought he would *totally* get it, you know, because of his raging alcoholism.

By the time I met my husband, I was stuck in a quagmire, my gift-giving fire quenched by a series of grueling relationships that had left me battered and weak. My mojo was gone, and my awesome gifts were universally despised. As it turns out, most people just want gift certificates, not turn-of-the-century dentists' tools or vintage carpet beaters.

I didn't know what to get Jason for the first birthday of his that we spent together. I had grown so unused to intimate gestures that I finally settled on a book, *Song of Solomon*, and a massage. Having had no experience with the latter, I booked him a massage at a local massage parlor. When the slinky gentleman emerged from his dank cave to accept my money and fashion an impromptu gift certificate, he eyed me warily. He must have thought I was the coolest girlfriend in the world.

I was like, "Great! A *guy* massage! Jason will feel so much more comfortable having a *guy* massage him." Perhaps I should have said each thought out loud to myself, articulating every syllable just so. "A. GUY. MASSAGE. JASON. WILL. FEEL. SO. MUCH. MORE. COMFORT-ABLE. HAVING. A. DUDE. RUB. HIM. DOWN. WITH. PINE. SCENTED. OIL. IN. A. DARK. MANCAVE. RUB-BING. HIM. ALL. OVER. WITH. HIS. BIG. MANLY. MEATPAWS."

Oh.

It was so traumatic for him that he didn't let on for years that he had, in fact, been molested in that bears' den. So sweet of him not to let on. He just told me it was great and that he loved it and, when pressed for more details, didn't seem to have much to say. Also, he hated the book and never read it. He only likes books that relate in some way to trage-dies that befall climbers on Mount Everest.

I swore I could do better. I knew I had it in me to *wow* him. After all, Jason had consistently wowed me at every possible holiday and birthday. He's the kind of person who remembers every single thing you've ever said about any-thing you've ever liked or wanted to do, and files it away in a steel trap in his brain in order to make you cry six months later. If he has to special-order it from blind orphans in Afghanistan, all the better to amaze you.

It took me ages to figure out, but I came up with a great idea. I decided to take Jason to an authentic dude ranch and give him the opportunity to rope cows and ride horses and do dude things that did not involve intimate rubdowns by guys in loose-fitting kimonos. Jason loves horses, and he's super-outdoorsy. Perfect.

I researched the idea for months and found the perfect place. It was only a few hours away, and it had all of the features I was looking for in a backcountry experience: off-trail horseback riding with actual duties, such as herding cattle into their pens; rustic Mexican blankets strewn across simple beds; coffee percolating on an open fire; and eating baked beans out of tins! The place came recommended in several of my urban-lifestyle magazines, and plus, all the lettering on the website had that burnt-edge *Bonanza* look to it. I was sold. We were going to herd cattle all day, rest our weary bones on some rusty old cots at night, then get up in the morning for some grub and do it all over again. He was going to love it. I mean, what the hell. I love horses, too, and I'm no slouch in the saddle, so I figured it was something we could both enjoy.

The guy on the phone was slightly lacking in customer-service skills, but I thought maybe that was just part of the act, like when you eat at Crabby Joe's and the waiters are all supposed to be mean to you on purpose. He called himself Kowboy Kevin, and when I asked him if they accepted American Express, he kind of snorted and I thought I heard him call me a "citi-ot."

I kind of chuckled, like, *I get it. It's all part of the rustic experience. Yes, I'm a "citi-ot."* But then I really needed to know. "So . . . heh, heh . . . *do* you take American Express?"

"No, your ladyship, we don't. We *don't* take American Express."

"Ummm . . . what *do* you take, Kowboy Kevin?"

"Cash only. No exceptions. Not for you, not for the Queen of England, and not for no Richie Rich and Lyle." Then he made a sound like he was blowing his nose into his hand. He sounded so authentic and musty. I hoped he was the one who was going to be taking us out on the range!

I put down my deposit, and when I told Jason about his gift, he *was* impressed by my ingenuity, and probably relieved that he wasn't getting a seventeenth-century merkin in a shadowbox or something. We got a babysitter for our dog, as the website had warned us that their nursing cows would try and trample her to death if we brought her, and took off, full of promise.

By the time we made our way up the long driveway to the main house, everything we owned was covered in about an inch and a half of dust, 90 percent of which I had to assume was desiccated manure. Of course, like complete assholes, we couldn't quite make out which driveway we were supposed to pull into, because for some reason it was really confusing and there appeared to be more than one. So essentially, we made our presence known by driving across the lawn for a quarter of a mile. Kowboy Kevin was not amused, and his various wild dogs were going ballistic in the yard. All of them seemed to have at least one eyeball or ear part missing; they were all in tatters, standing around in a minefield of dried poop, chained to spare tires. When I stepped into the yard, a giant, hissing, dirty white goose advanced on me aggressively, backing me up against the car with its enormous, filthy flapping wings. Geese really hate me.

Kevin was there to greet us, of course, but he was so mad that we messed up our entrance that he could barely look us in the eye. His wife and children ambled out of the back of the house and somehow seemed even less enthusiastic than Kevin to see us. It was like we had driven unannounced up to the doorway of a survivalist compound in New Hampshire. Here we were in Kevinland, and there were paranoid hand-made signs nailed to all the trees saying things like, PARK SERVICE—KEEP OUT! and TRESPASSERS WILL BE SHOT ON SIGHT! It was not very welcoming.

So far, it was lacking in the dude-ranch *je ne sais quoi* that I had been hoping for. I was thinking faux rustic, but this was actually just rustic. And by rustic, of course, I mean awful. For some reason, the website didn't fully com-municate the reality of the living situation at Kowboy Kev-in's. These people didn't seem to want to take in city people and give them a slice of the romantic ranch-hand way of life at all. In my mind I started going through the people I had told of our adventure, and wondered how long it would take for them to start looking for our bodies once we disappeared.

Kevin's wife reluctantly took us to our bunkie, which at least gave us some relief from the children boring their eyes into the backs of our skulls. On the way there, I happened to glance at my dented Neon. In contrast to the rusted-out vehi-cle graveyard it was parked in, it looked futuristic and luxuri-ous, like I had driven my priceless moon pod to this backwater junk heap to rub it in everyone's faces. Even my car looked uncomfortable sitting there with those weird children staring at her.

We agreed to meet at the stable in an hour, and one of the children took our sandwich order, which was really just, "Do you want a sandwich, or not?" I had already started apologizing to Jason for how bad I knew this was going to be, but he clung to his optimism. I mean, at least we were going to be riding horses, right? And in the end, we were sort of helping a family get a leg up, which was good. How bad could it be?

Kevin had a little boot camp that he would put people through before deciding which horse they would get to ride for the day. It involved a series of questions and activities that would help him determine your level of confidence on horseback, and whether he could trust you not to have to wear a helmet.

Jason passed with flying colors. He's kind of a big guy, and he's very confident about his horseback-riding abilities. I, on the other hand, am small, and I always forget that there are actually some physical activities that I am capable of doing without too much trouble. Also, I don't like to overestimate my skill set, so when Kevin asked me how experienced I was with horses, I wasn't sure how to answer. I mean, my mom had a farm, so I had actually had quite a bit of riding experience. But it had been a while, so I didn't want to make it seem like I was amazing at it, even though I secretly thought I was. My plan had been to work my way into Kowboy Kevin's good graces by acting really modest at first and then suddenly impressing him with my equestrian prowess.

He instantly assessed my skill level at "zero." I pointed out that that wasn't factually accurate, that I had ridden many horses in my time and none of them had taken the upper hand with me. It was no use. I had wavered, and he took my lack of confidence to mean that anything I said was just a face-saving lie and that I was not to be trusted. He left us standing there by ourselves and returned ten minutes later with a hot pink bicycle helmet and a straw cowboy hat.

"Put these on."

"Oh, no," I protested. "No, thanks. I'm really going to be fine. As I mentioned, I'm actually quite good on horse-back . . . I just haven't done it in a while—"

"We're not going anywhere until you put these on."

Jason chimed in, "No. Really. She does know what she's doing—"

Kevin sighed. I couldn't believe how much he hated us, and he had just met us. We hadn't even given him a proper chance to hate us yet.

"I said, we're not going anywhere until you put these on. I'm not getting sued if you fall off the horse and crack your skull wide open and spill your brains all over a jagged rock. I can't take the chance."

I could see that I wasn't getting anywhere with him, so I gave up. "Well, which one do you want me to wear, then?"

"Both. This one's for safety, the other one's for decor."

I grudgingly put on the bicycle helmet, which was the

most out-of-date model remaining in existence. It was the kind that had a big loop on the top that could be attached to a rope line, so that if you were severely mentally disabled, you could go in the backyard and run back and forth without anyone fearing that you could get away or hurt yourself. "But it doesn't even fit me—"

Then Kevin jammed that cowboy hat on top of the helmet. "The horses don't like the pink color. Spooks them."

The width of the bicycle helmet expanded the base of the cowboy hat, so it looked insane on my head. I looked like an encephalitic child going for the last ride of my life through the good work of the Children's Miracle Network. Tears were streaming out of Jason's eyes. He turned his back and I could see his shoulders shuddering with laughter.

Then Kevin took us over to his proving ground, which was basically one of those big blue water coolers attached at both ends to a large wooden frame by a network of ropes and knots. We were supposed to mount the water cooler, so he could see if we were capable of staying upright on a horse. Of course, Jason nailed it. His legs were long enough to entwine at the underside of the cooler and he was able to tighten his thighs sufficiently so as not to slip off.

I, on the other hand, could not entwine my legs under the water cooler. I pointed out that this was not an accurate simulation of the experience of being in a saddle. There was nothing but the slippery blue surface of the plastic to sit on, and anyway, a person could never hold on to a horse by entwining one's legs underneath it. It just didn't work for me.

"Just do it."

Kowboy Kevin was really beginning to annoy me.

"Fine, but I just fail to see what this has to do with—"

Suddenly, he started violently pulling on the ropes. I pitched forward, my protective headgear immediately slipped off to one side, and I smashed my face into the rope, giving myself a rope burn that extended all the way from below my chin to the top of my forehead. I started to cry.

"Why did you *do* that? Oh my *God*!" Jason was so mad. I could tell he was starting to feel guilty about laughing at the helmet situation. "See! I *told* you that helmet was useless! It fell right off!"

I was sweaty, covered in dust, and crying with a big red burn mark on my face that was bleeding a little bit where it had been rubbed the most violently. I dabbed at it tenderly with a tissue. I looked like I had just gotten kicked off the short bus for starting a fight club.

I wanted to leave so badly and I could tell that Jason did, too. But we are both Canadian, and that means that we are required by nature to stick it out politely, and then talk about it incessantly after the fact. So we both took a deep breath and prepared to receive our horse assignments.

Jason naturally got the prize stallion. He was tall and impressive, a picture-perfect horse, black and shiny with a long, well-groomed mane and tail, and nostrils that flared just so. I couldn't believe *that* horse came out of *that* barn. All of

Jason's reservations and feelings of empathy were instantly whisked away, as he imagined himself whipping across the field atop this glorious mount.

I was naturally assigned to the horse that was three inches from death, clearly on her last mission before being dispatched to the dog-food factory. Her name was Buttercup, for God's sake. I had no idea what Kevin had been so concerned about. This horse was so old and fat she could barely walk, much less buck me off onto the jagged rocks below. She was practically a cow. The only thing I had to fear was the possibility that she would expire while we were out and squash me underneath her hulking weight.

We were off.

I spent the whole ride looking at the ass end of Kevin's and Jason's horses as they gamely trotted ahead. Mine seemed to enjoy stopping to look at things, sneezing, and trying to get me off of her by pretending to stumble and rubbing herself against trees. I would have liked to have been able to point out to everyone else that it actually took much greater skill to get such a lazy horse to move forward and listen to commands, but they were so far ahead of me that it was impossible. Still, the quiet was nice, and it was a beautiful day, so I was having a rather pleasant time and had calmed down considerably since the water cooler incident.

Then we went up a hill and into a clearing where there were some cows scattered around. Suddenly Kevin started yelling at us. I could barely make out what he was saying because he was so far ahead of me, but he seemed to be indicating that we needed to round the cows up? I wasn't really sure. So I started trotting toward a little group of cows. *This must be the fun part,* I thought, *where we pretend to round up the cows a little bit,* and I started getting into it. Even Buttercup seemed to be enjoying herself.

That's when I saw Kevin barreling toward me, yelling in German, of all things. *"Beeil dich! Schnell!"*

What the hell? What kind of dude ranch was this guy running? It was all happening so quickly, I started to get very confused. And worried. What if Krazy Kevin had sold us on a vacation that was really just a ploy to imprison us in a Terezín-style transit work camp before shipping us off to meet our maker? I just sat there on my horse, frozen.

"Was machen Sie, Samantha! *Was machen Sie?"*

"What? *What?* I don't speak German! What are you saying?" We were calling to each other across the field.

"The *cows,* you *idiot.* They're *getting away!*"

As far as I could tell, the cows were just kind of standing there, looking very relaxed.

Jason raced over and started yelling at Kowboy Kevin, too. He had given us no warning that we were about to herd cows, he didn't tell us where he wanted them, and we couldn't see any pens anywhere near us. We were just two people sitting on horses in the middle of an open field with Kowboy Kevin shouting at us in the native language of the Nazis.

"Fuck, Saman-za! *Fuck!*" His German accent literally came out of nowhere. I was so pissed off, but also, still very confused. *"Pass auf, du Trampeltier! Mein Gott,* Samanza! *Fuck!"*

I had had it.

"No, *fuck you, you fucker!*" I shouted after him. *"Don't you swear at me! Leave me the fuck alone, you fucker—face!"* Sometimes when I get really mad at people, I just start saying the F-word indiscriminately. He continued to yell about me as he took off after the cows, though I couldn't make out what he was saying. Still, I wanted to get the last word.

"For *the fuck of . . . hell! Your website is misleading! You stupid German . . . person! You should get a new pamphlet that says 'I will cut your face if you come here.' Motherfucker!"*

By then the cows were running haphazardly toward something far off in the distance, and Kowboy Kevin was in hot pursuit. If I had been one of his cows, I would have run for my life, too.

I was very tired of getting sworn at by this angry stranger, and I knew that the things he was saying about me in German were much worse than the things I could comprehend in English. I had no idea why he thought I would instinctively know how to do this. I certainly hadn't done anything to impress him up to that point, so I wasn't entirely sure why he had left the rounding up of the cows in my court.

I sidled up to Jason and we agreed that we had to leave immediately. I now knew that our lives were in danger or, at the very least, that Jason was about to get in a fistfight with a weird farmer man. My skin was crawling; I wanted to get out of there so badly. When we told Kevin's wife that we were leaving early, she tried to appear confused, but you could tell she knew the score. Nobody had to tell her she had married Hitler's forgotten half-brother.

"But you paid for the deluxe overnighter . . . don't you want any baked beans? Or a sandwich?" She sighed and started to wrap our food in cellophane for the car. The Children of the Corn eyed us eerily from across the yard.

As we peeled out of the driveway, our egos (and one of our faces) battered and bruised, I burst into tears. We sat in silence for most of the way home, eating our warm sandwiches, while I wondered if Jason could ever think of me sexually again, having seen me in that cowboy helmet. I wished for a time machine to return his memory to a pre-headgear image of me, but I knew that his mind was like a bear trap, and that in every ensuing intimate moment, I would feel a slight undercurrent of shame.

If the relationship lasted through his next birthday, I decided, I'd get him a lovely cerulean V-neck cashmere sweater wrapped in glossy lime green paper with a brown organza ribbon. He doesn't know it yet, but cerulean really brings out the color of his eyes.

After all, it's the thought that counts.

acknowledgments

Thanks to Tricia for your lovely work and patience. To Jay, to Brian, and to all of the people at Simon & Schuster who know how a semicolon is supposed to work, because I certainly don't. Is this; right;?

Thank you to Jon Stewart and all of the wonderful people at *The Daily Show*, who have been loving and supportive at every step along the way. This cannot be overstated. I still can't believe I get to work with all of you every day.

As an underachiever in the field of "coming up with titles," I would like to extend a special thank-you to those who helped me figure out what to call this thing. I'm looking at you, Tim Carvell. And you too, Jim Margolis, whose *Greetings from the Future Mrs. Simon Le Bon* will always remain my sentimental favorite.

Thanks to my mother, my father, and my stepmother. I love you all dearly. To my grandfather, who recently passed away, wherever you are, thank you for teaching me about charity and doing it with such panache. And to my grandmother, whom I miss so much it still makes my bones ache. What the hell were you thinking, dying on me like that?

Finally, to my husband, Jason. I'm not even going to try and be funny with it, because I just love you. Thank you for listening to me go on and on about "process" when really I was just scared shitless to put out a book. And to my children: It's going to get annoying hearing me say this over and over again for your entire lives, but I love you *this much*. Infinity.